# Habitual Peace

Transform Your Life with Daily Dhikr Habits For Big Rewards in this Dunya and the Akhirah

SARAH GULFRAZ

Copyright © 2025 Sarah Gulfraz

Sarah Gulfraz has asserted her right to be identified as the author of this Work in accordance with the Copyright, Designs and Patents Act 1988.

All rights reserved.

No portion of this book may be reproduced in any form, stored in a retrieval system, stored in a database, or published/transmitted in any form or by any means, electronic, mechanical, photocopying, recording or otherwise, without prior written permission of the publisher.

# Dedication

**~ Bismillah ~**

May Allah (swt) accept our efforts and grant us success in this life and the next. Ameen.

In dedication to my loving family and all their support.

# Contents

1. Introduction   1
2. Introduction to Dhikr   4
3. The Spiritual and Emotional Impact of Dhikr   12
4. The Dhikr Practices of the Prophet Muhammad (PBUH)   19
5. Developing a Daily Dhikr Routine   31
6. Dhikr and Its Role in Personal Transformation   38
7. Integrating Dhikr into Different Aspects of Life   48
8. The Benefits of Dhikr for Physical Health   61
9. Overcoming Challenges in Maintaining a Dhikr Habit   68
10. The Impact of Dhikr on the Akhirah (Hereafter)   81
11. Embracing Dhikr as a Lifelong Practice   93
12. Conclusion   100

Find Out More   102

# Chapter One

# Introduction

Peace of mind and calm are the primary aspirations of every human being, particularly during a time when we are racing with the world to accomplish all of the material goals that we establish for ourselves or that society places on us. Sometimes life can be too much to handle. Many of us feel cut off from the world and from our faith because of our work, family, and personal commitments. In our hearts, we yearn for a deeper relationship with Allah (SWT), one that allows us to sense His presence guiding us through difficulties and sharing in our happiness.

The good news is that it is possible to deepen your relationship with Allah (SWT), which can improve your daily life and provide you with clarity, comfort, and serenity.

Dhikr, one of the primary means of reaching a higher spiritual state, is the process of becoming closer to Allah (SWT) through various forms of worship and meditation. It is more than just repeating specific phrases; it is a way to achieve inner peace, spiritual purity, and intimacy with the Creator. Remembering Allah (SWT) has several advantages and a significant impact. It gives spirits and hearts a place to relax and keeps ills at bay. In this life as well as the next, it brings believers contentment and prosperity. A sincere believer's enjoyment is more integrated the more he dedicates himself to remembering Allah (SWT).

Without remembrance, the reality of hearts in this worldly life is incredibly complex and full of desires, attraction by lusts, suspicions, and seditions. It suggests that these hearts are restless, irritated, and disoriented, harbouring suspicions and doubts within them. Without remembering Allah (SWT), no heart can be at peace. The key query is how to get inner peace and tranquillity, which is something that everyone aspires to. In the words of the Quran, Allah Almighty (SWT) provides an answer to this query.

> *"Those who believe, and whose hearts find rest in the remembrance of Allah. Verily, in the remembrance of Allah do hearts find rest" (Quran 13:28)*

According to Islamic teachings, Dhikr is considered a crucial spiritual practice that boosts faith and improves the bond between people and Allah (SWT). This book is not just about rituals or routines; it is about transformation. It is about becoming who you are truly meant to be through the powerful and divine practice of Dhikr—the remembrance of Allah (SWT).

Individuals seeking a deeper connection with Allah (SWT) are the target audience for this book. Through the holy practice of Dhikr, or remembering the Creator, this life-changing adventure leads you to awaken your heart. You'll gain a deep insight that is necessary for a spiritual connection by reading this book, and elevate your relationship with the Divine by imprinting love into your soul via the practice of Dhikr.

You'll see how consistently reciting Dhikr brings divine blessings into every aspect of your life through this immersive experience as you integrate these holy words into your daily life, recite, commit to memory, and cultivate a Dhikr habit through repetition. This book seeks to encourage you to adopt these sayings in your everyday life and open up the countless benefits that lie ahead by providing you with insights, advice, and several forms of Dhikr to study.

This book aims to guide all, whether you're someone who is already familiar with this practice or someone who is just ready to take initiative to explore its beauty; you are welcome here. All you need is your pure intention and, most importantly, your desire to grow closer to Allah (SWT).

You'll learn the beauty and meaning of every term, as well as its rewards and advantages in this life and the next, within the pages of this book. Explore the depths of thankfulness, find comfort in asking for pardon, and take in the wonder of Allah's (SWT) presence.

# Chapter Two

# Introduction to Dhikr

## Understanding Dhikr: Remembrance of Allah (SWT)

The existence of Allah (SWT) is not a blind faith, a fantasy, or a dogma. It is the expression of this world's actuality and truth. Allah (SWT) is seen and observable in the universe's creation. The existence of Allah (SWT) is the Absolute Truth and Reality, as evidenced by the beauty of everything in this universe and the system that exists within it. Our ability to reason, perceive the world, and be inspired is adequate to attest to the veracity and unquestionability of Allah's (SWT) existence.

Everyone must acknowledge the presence of Allah (SWT) and submit to Him. Whether we like it or not, it is a fact of life that we must all come back to Him. He is immortal, and we are mortal. The Rule of Law, which we all believe to be essential to society and life, requires that we return to Allah (SWT), give an account of our lives, and experience justice. Thus, building our relationship with Allah (SWT) ought to be our first goal in life.

Remembering Allah (SWT) brings to mind our Creator, the origin of all beauty and goodness. As an illustration, when someone views a stunning painting or reads a remarkable poem or book, their heart wants to meet the creator. We experience awe and affection for the creator because we know that they must be even more wonderful than the object we see. Furthermore, Allah (SWT) is far superior to these comparisons. When we encounter and observe the creation around us, our hearts naturally sense love, awe, and a desire to recall and reflect on Allah (SWT). This is a natural expression of the heart.

Being a Muslim, we're aware that remembrance of Allah (SWT) is one of the most profound and spiritually nourishing acts in Islam. We are also aware that Dhikr is present in everything around us. Everything—the planets, the trees, the seas, the wind, the animals, and the universe—was made in a condition of 'Ubudiyyah,' or surrender to the worship of Allah (SWT), and is done in His honour. We are placing ourselves in a position of harmony and union with creation when we are in Dhikr.

Dhikr encompasses a wide range of practices designed to maintain the believer's connection with their Creator, keeping it alive and strong. It transcends rituals and becomes a way of life—transforming mundane routines into moments of divine connection. In a world full of distractions, Dhikr serves as a sanctuary for the soul, a place where the heart finds peace, and it brings clarity, comfort, and an enduring sense of purpose.

## Definition and Significance of Dhikr in Islam

The Arabic term Dhikr, which implies remembering or mentioning, has a plural form, Adhkar. However, in the Islamic context, it refers to remembering and mentioning Allah (SWT), which is worship and simply praising Allah (SWT) and exalting Him verbally and internally. Since Allah (SWT) created the entire world and is ultimately in control of all time, one of the fundamental tenets of Islam is to rely on Him in all facets of life and ask Him for strength, support, and direction. Adhkar is a similar and crucial form of prayer.

Believers' minds and spirits get calmer, their conviction grows, and their faith deepens when they perform the Dhikr of Allah (SWT). All good, happiness, delight, pleasure, and tranquilly in this world and the next are dependent on the performance of the Dhikr of Allah (SWT); in fact, all laws and acts of obedience were enacted to establish the Dhikr of Allah (SWT). The Dhikr of Allah (SWT) is the sign of happiness and the route to success in this world and the hereafter.

> *Once a man asked Messenger of Allah (PBUH), "Which Jihad is greater in reward?" He replied: "The one in which they make the most Dhikr of Allah." (SWT). He [then] asked: "Who from amongst those fasting are greater in reward?" He said: "The ones who make Dhikr of Allah (SWT) —the most." Then he mentioned to us the Saldh, Zakdli, Hajj and Sadaqah (charity) and the Messenger of Allah (SWT) would say regarding all of them: "The ones that are most in making Dhikr of Allah" (SWT). So Abu Bakr said to 'Umar: "O Abu Hafs the Dhakirun (the ones that make Dhikr) have taken all the good." The Messenger of Allah— replied: "Certainly!" (Musnad Ahmad)*

Abounding bounties and great rewards in this world and the next—whose count cannot be enumerated but by Allah (SWT)—are a direct result of Dhikr, which is the soul, the life of the heart, and the cause of its development and power. Salah, fasting, the Hajj, and other acts of obedience are mandated for Allah's (SWT) servants, and their purpose is to establish memory of Allah (SWT) alone. Therefore, the Dhakiriin are the ones who deserve to receive the greatest honours, the highest positions, and the highest stations in paradise.

## Quranic and Hadith references highlighting its importance

Muslims who recite Dhikr and remember Allah (SWT) with their hearts and words reap several rewards.

> *Allah (SWT) tells us in the Quran: "O you who believe! Remember Allah with much remembrance" (Quran 33:41)*

> *The Prophet (PBUH) said: "Keep your tongue wet with the remembrance of Allah." (Tirmidhi)*

> *The Prophet (PBUH) also told us: "He who remembers his Lord and he who do not are like the living and the dead." (Bukhari)*

In the light of the Quran, below are a few benefits of remembering Allah (SWT) that Muslims must know:

> *"O ye who believe! Celebrate the praises of Allah, and do this often; and glorify Him morning and evening." (Quran 41-42:33)*

Forgiveness and a substantial recompense are guaranteed to those who perform Dhikr and remember Allah (SWT) frequently.

> *"... And for men and women who engage much in Allah's praise,- for them has prepared forgiveness and great reward." (Quran 35:33)*

Peace and tranquillity are brought to the heart by dedicating your tongue and heart to Dhikr:

> *"Those who believe, and whose hearts find satisfaction in the remembrance of Allah: for without doubt in the remembrance of Allah do hearts find satisfaction." (Quran 28:13)*

The Muslim becomes closer to Allah (SWT) through Dhikr and receives the honour from Allah (SWT). The Messenger of Allah (PBUH) said:

> *"Allah the Exalted says: 'I am as my slave expects me to be, and I am with him when he remembers Me. If he remembers Me inwardly, I will remember him inwardly, and if he remembers Me in an assembly, I will remember him in a better assembly (i.e., in the assembly of angels)" (Sahih Muslim)*

Dhikr is a wonderful chance to deepen your relationship with Allah (SWT) get closer to Him, and experience serenity and security in His presence.

## Dhikr is a Source of Serenity for the Hearts

The genuine vitality of the heart is Dhikr, and without it, they will perish. Those who remember Allah (SWT) are alive, and those who do not remember Allah (SWT) are dead. These are two examples provided by the Prophet (PBUH).

> *Allah (SWT) says in the Quran: ... "the Day when neither wealth nor children will be of any benefit. Only those who come before Allah with a pure heart will be saved" (Quran 26:88–89)*

As the secret to our prosperity in the Hereafter, the verse above highlights the need to clean our hearts in this life. This passage states that on the Day of Judgement, having a pure heart will be our only asset and that our money and children will be useless.

As believers, we urgently need to turn back to Allah (SWT) and concentrate on heart and soul purification. Diseased hearts are the primary cause of many of the world's issues. These hearts lack knowledge of Allah (SWT) and are conceited, avaricious, and self-centred. The pleasure of iman is no longer tasted by hearts that have been tainted by sin. Pride, envy, and hatred tear apart the hearts of the Ummah, causing it to become fragmented.

A dead heart worships others and turns away from its Creator and Lord. In times of hope, desire, fear, love, and hatred, it does not follow Allah's (SWT) commands and does not beg for help from Him. We Muslims must answer this challenge and work to rid our hearts of vices as immorality, hatred, envy, worldliness, greed, and conceit. Positive attributes like thankfulness, kindness, generosity, and compassion should take the place of these negative ones.

A heart that is free of illnesses and malign intent is said to be sound. The actions are cleansed, and it is purified for Allah's (SWT) sake. As a result, this person worships Allah (SWT) alone, turns solely to Him, and depends on Him. If it loves, it does so for Allah's (SWT) sake; if it dislikes, it does so for Allah's (SWT) sake. It is a pure heart, free of lusts and illnesses. It is closer to Allah (SWT) by remembering Him and worshipping Him alone.

Both life and death are present in the third kind of heart. When it is sincere, true, monotheistic, and desirous of worshipping Allah (SWT), it is charged with life; when it is lustful and suspicious, it lacks this vitality. Depending on the dominating drive, the heart is classified as either dead or alive. When one stays closer to Allah (SWT) and recalls Allah (SWT) with his heart and speech, suspicions and lusts are eliminated, and the life of the heart is sustained.

There would be illnesses if one does not remember Allah (SWT). How do these hearts find rest? By submitting to Allah (SWT), depending on Him, and turning to Him alone. Anyone who prays to Allah (SWT) alone, hopes for Allah (SWT) alone, fears Allah (SWT) alone, and relies on Allah (SWT) alone knows that his heart is secure in remembering Allah (SWT) for performing Tawheed and following Allah (SWT) in all circumstances.

## Dhikr Repels the Devil

With the Dhikr of Allah (SWT), a person stays in a powerful shelter and an impenetrable fortress that the devil cannot enter, pushing the devil away from the believer. A Hadith that the Prophet (PBUH) stated is recorded by Imam 'Ahmad in al-Musnad and by others with a reliable chain of narration:

> *"Verily, Allah (SWT) — commanded Yahya Zakariyya (AS) with commandments to abide by, and to command the Children of Isra'il to abide by them" (Tirmidhi)*

> *Zakariyya (AS) told his followers: "Verily, my Lord instructed me with five commandments, and He ordered me to instruct you with it." Then he mentioned the command firstly with Tawhid (singling Allah SWT alone in worship), Salah, charity, then he mentioned the fifth command: command with the Dhikr of Allah (SWT), so he said: "I command you to make the remembrance of Allah (SWT) in abundance; and verily, the similitude of this is like a man who is quickly tracked by the enemy, so he comes to an impenetrable fortress and seeks protection from it. And the most fortified a servant can be*

*from the devil is if he is occupied with the Dhikr of Allah (SWT)" (Tirmidhi)*

Therefore, the person who performs Dhikr of Allah (SWT) is in an impregnable stronghold and a powerful shelter that the devil can never enter. Satan retreats, flinches, and transforms into a fly when the servant makes Dhikr of his Lord. He will not stay with the person doing Dhikr; instead, he will run away from him. He finds it unbearable to listen to Allah's (SWT) Dhikr. In reality, the Dhikr hurts and drives him away, and he separates himself from a location where the Dhikr of Allah (SWT) is done. But if he (the servant) is careless, the devils will approach him one after the other, lead him to deception, and nudge him hard to sin.

*"And whosoever turns away blindly from the remembrance of the Most Gracious (Allah) (i.e. this Quran and worship of Allah), we appoint for him Shaitan (Satan) to be a Qarln (an intimate companion) to him" (Quran 43:36)*

The devil will stay away from you if you offer Dhikr of Allah (SWT) just before you eat, if you offer Dhikr of Allah (SWT) as soon as you enter your home, and so on. In this way, the devil will be unable to reach you in any situation where you offer Dhikr of Allah (SWT), and you will be shielded from his satanic poetry, evil, prodding, whispers, and schemes.

# Chapter Three

# The Spiritual and Emotional Impact of Dhikr

## Enhancing Spiritual Connection

Dhikr has innumerable benefits including spiritual, emotional, and psychological perks of practicing Dhikr. Spirituality fosters a person's spiritual connection with Allah (SWT), cultivating closeness and an understanding of His presence. Additionally, Dhikr has a relaxing impact on the mind and body on an emotional and psychological level, assisting in the regulation of emotions, lowering tension and anxiety, fostering inner peace, and cultivating contentment and thankfulness. Muslims can enhance their overall well-being and experience a profound sense of peace and spiritual fulfilment by incorporating Dhikr into their daily lives. Now let's take a closer look at its advantages, and more!

## Spiritual Rewards of Dhikr

Dhikr can be a powerful fortification in the face of global catastrophe by bolstering people's morals and spirituality, making them more prudent in their behaviour, and preserving the harmony of social connections and the natural world. Dhikr plays a crucial role in overcoming the various modern obstacles that can jeopardise the spiritual equilibrium of people. Dhikr is a technique that can bring inner peace, quiet the soul, and lessen worry. One can feel calmer and more at ease by diverting their attention from tension and unpleasant thoughts by concentrating on the words of remembering.

In today's often materialistic world, remembering helps maintain a balance between the material and spiritual facets of life. One's faith and spirituality can be strengthened by always remembering Allah (SWT), which helps one deal with worldly temptations and lead a balanced life. Additionally, Dhikr might enhance the calibre of one's worship. When conducting other acts of worship, Dhikr helps one become more serious and focused. This is significant because high-quality worship can offer profound spiritual fulfilment and mental tranquillity.

## Deepening Relationship with Allah (SWT) through Consistent Dhikr

Dhikr is a means of seeking spiritual enlightenment and establishing a connection with Allah (SWT) in Islamic mysticism. It enables believers to remember Allah's (SWT) presence in their lives and concentrate their thoughts on His qualities. Muslims seek to deepen their relationship with Allah (SWT) and attain inner serenity through Dhikr. By pleading for pardon for previous transgressions and seeking direction on the road of righteousness, Dhikr is said to bring blessings into one's life. By reminding people that they are not alone and have a divine relationship with Allah (SWT), who is always present, it offers consolation during trying times.

Most Islamic scholars concur that iman (faith) is dynamic, rising when one obeys Allah's (SWT) precepts and falling when one disobeys. Therefore, acquiring Iman is a process. Just because someone is a Muslim by birth or conversion does not mean that it enters their heart. Allah (SWT) grants Iman to those who honestly strive for it because of His mercy. Iman is made up of our body's limbs acting in certain ways, our tongue making a message, and our heart's belief. Gaining, preserving, and growing our iman must be among our objectives as Muslims. We need to foster and safeguard our religion. It needs to be fed the things that will keep it alive. Like the early Muslims, who frequently questioned the Prophet (PBUH) about the state of their faith, we should be troubled by it all the time. The Prophet (PBUH) said, according to Abu Huraira, may Allah (SWT) be pleased with him:

> *"Renew your faith."* The companions asked, *"How can we renew our faith?"* The Prophet replied, *"Say always, 'La ilaha ilAllah' (there is none worthy of worship except Allah)."* (Musnad Ahmad)

## Emotional and Other Benefits of Dhikr

Dhikr offers major advantages for mental health as well. The symptoms of depression and other mental illnesses can be lessened with regular Dhikr practice. This is because Dhikr can offer a profound sense of joy, happiness, and security—all of which are linked to improved mental well-being. People are encouraged to discover their own selves and their relationship with Allah (SWT) through Dhikr. This helps prevent a person from developing heart and soul problems and balances their physical, biological, and spiritual needs. As a result, Dhikr aids people in finding contentment and mental tranquillity.

Dhikr is a source of solace for hearts. Why? This is the case because anxiety arises when a person believes that a disaster is going to destroy him; if he is positive that there is a cure for every disaster and illness, he will not experience worry. Therefore, when a person remembers Allah (SWT) and realises that Allah (SWT) has boundless power and can cure any illness, his heart reminds him that if he has such an Allah (SWT), why should he worry about anything? He will take it off himself. He gets solace in this way. When overcoming obstacles in life, Dhikr develops a strong and robust mindset. A person will feel more protected and be highly motivated to take action and overcome a variety of obstacles in life as they get closer to Allah (SWT).

It is impossible to overlook the significance of integrating intellectual thought with spiritual remembering. People frequently become engrossed in logical, scientific thinking that can overlook the spiritual side of things when confronted with modernity. A strong foundation of self is formed in the face of life's challenges when thought and Dhikr are integrated to assist in establishing a balance between intellect and spirituality. Therefore, Dhikr plays a crucial part in conquering the different modern obstacles that can jeopardise the spiritual equilibrium of people.

## Cultivating Positive Emotions and Resilience through Dhikr

Muslims are urged by the Quran to cultivate strong, resilient personalities that persevere through hardships.

> "*Indeed, those who have said, 'Our Lord is Allah' and then remained steadfast—the angels will descend upon them, [saying], 'Do not fear and do not grieve but receive good tidings of Paradise, which you were promised'*" (Quran 41:30)

Believers are reassured by this verse that negative emotions such as fear and grief do not solve problems and should not stand in the way of advancement. Dhikr, the remembrance of Allah (SWT), plays a transformative role in nurturing positive emotions and building resilience.

This spiritual practice involves the repeated recitation of specific phrases or names of Allah (SWT), which helps calm the mind and soothe the heart. Engaging in Dhikr regularly allows individuals to shift their focus away from stressors and negative thoughts, grounding them in the present moment and fostering a sense of inner peace.

We can see that anxiety in the heart is the root cause of many emotional issues. Dhikr helps calm the heart and soul in this circumstance. Confusion and concentrated thoughts can cause someone to become extremely exhausted. By praying to Allah (SWT) and pursuing spiritual enlightenment, religious techniques help people deepen their spiritual convictions. The conviction that Allah (SWT) is the only source of assurance and a cure for all illnesses ultimately emerges in these situations.

The understanding that challenges have always existed in human life and that every person changes over the course of their lifetime means that when a person confronts his issues with Allah (SWT), he will experience issues at the level of his emotional intelligence, feeling hopeless, perplexed, and even dangerous if his heart is not filled with the memory of Allah (SWT). Emotional anxiety can be eliminated by prayer and remembering. Repeatedly remembering Allah (SWT) is a form of worship that keeps us in tune with him and allows us to live fully conscious lives. The repetition of divine words not only strengthens faith but also encourages mindfulness, gratitude, and emotional balance.

Through Dhikr, believers are reminded of Allah's (SWT) mercy, compassion, and wisdom, which instil hope during difficult times. This connection to the Divine enables individuals to endure hardship with patience and trust, thereby contributing to their emotional resilience. By internalising these positive affirmations, practitioners are better equipped to cope with adversity, anxiety, and grief.

The spiritual strength gained from Dhikr acts as a buffer against emotional turbulence, promoting a stable and optimistic mindset. In essence, Dhikr is more than a ritual; it is a powerful tool for emotional well-being. It offers a pathway to contentment, reinforces a believer's trust in Allah's (SWT) plan, and fosters a resilient heart capable of facing life's challenges with courage and faith.

## Social and Community Impact of Dhikr

In addition to the spiritual rewards for the performer, Dhikr has a favourable social impact on society. Dhikr has several social effects, such as assisting in behaviour control in day-to-day interactions. One's behaviour in social situations can be influenced by ongoing factors. Regular Dhikr practitioners are generally more circumspect in both their words and deeds.

Dhikr eases the emotional strain caused by societal injustice and life's increasing demands. Finding inner calm through Dhikr makes one more capable of handling societal difficulties sensibly. Congregational Dhikr can strengthen community members' social bonds. Building a healthy community requires fostering a sense of unity and solidarity, which is what this exercise does.

Dhikr's awareness of Allah's (SWT) presence can keep people from sinning or engaging in bad habits that are detrimental to society. Therefore, Dhikr has a favourable effect on the social life of the community as a whole in addition to being advantageous to individuals. Dhikr fosters the development of a more virtuous, compassionate, and harmonious society. Dhikr helps people remember the moral principles and ethics that Islam teaches. In day-to-day social interactions, this promotes better and more responsible behaviour.

Additionally, the biggest advantage of performing Dhikr is that it brings Allah's (SWT) pleasure. If a servant remembers Allah (SWT), then Allah (SWT) becomes his friend. As Allah (SWT) says, O my servants! I'll remember you; you should remember me. And the only thing that Allah (SWT) Almighty remembers is that He gives everyone a chance to be heard. Allah (SWT) Almighty performs the same thing when he remembers someone, just as a worldly king would do when he calls that person into his court.

Man is protected from evil by remembering Allah (SWT) since it fortifies the heart and gives one the strength to resist evil. Man does not lose; instead, he remains resolute in the fight. Allah (SWT) instructs the Holy Prophet (PBUH) to establish Salah and recite the Quran, that Allah (SWT) has given to the people, as Salah protects against immorality and bad manifestation. Additionally, it is a very important virtue to remember Allah (SWT). Why? Because remembering Allah (SWT) is a powerful weapon, and when it strikes Satan's (devil) head, he becomes weaker and is unable to urge others to do evil.

> *Moreover, the Holy Prophet (PBUH) says that on the Day of Judgement, seven people will be under the shade of Allah (SWT), and among them will be the one who remembers Allah (SWT. (Tirmidhi)*

According to the Holy Prophet (PBUH), it will be such a perilous day that all prophets will be terrified, and Allah Almighty will be wrathful like never before, since all of the troublemakers will be brought before Him. The sun will get closer. One can only imagine how fortunate the person who receives the shade of Allah (SWT) on that day would be in light of this circumstance!

Therefore, before a man enters the presence of Allah (SWT), he should accept his humility as well as the strength and authority of Allah Almighty (SWT). It is a human rule that he develops a love for the thing he is always in contact with, to the point where he even starts to develop a love for the town or village where he lives. Thus, the love of Allah (SWT) gradually grows in a servant's heart when he recalls Allah (SWT) morning and evening—in fact, at all times—and says His name.

For those who are intelligent, the creation of the earth and heavens, as well as the cycle of day and night, includes several signs. Following that, it is said that those who continue to remember Allah (SWT) and reflect on His deeds are the ones who are intelligent. Thus, these are the advantages of remembering Allah (SWT) that were briefly discussed. May Allah Almighty benefit us all from them!

# Chapter Four

# The Dhikr Practices of the Prophet Muhammad (PBUH)

The Holy Prophet's commitment to and love for Allah (SWT) influenced every facet of his existence. The majority of his day and nighttime hours were devoted to worshipping and praising Almighty Allah, despite the exceptionally demanding duties that had been placed upon him. The Holy Prophet (PBUH) was constantly focused on remembering Allah (SWT). It was not confined to specific times or places; rather, it flowed naturally through his words, actions, and intentions.

Prophet Muhammad (PBUH) taught others how to conduct his religious deeds and carried them out in the most flawless way possible. Sincerity is the most crucial element that the Holy Quran highlights about the worship of the Prophet Muhammad (PBUH).

> *"Say (O Muhammad): O! I am commanded to worship Allah, making religion pure for Him only" (Quran 39:11), "Rather, worship Allah and be among the grateful" (Quran 39:66)*

Sincerity entails purging the heart of all idolatry and hypocrisy and focusing solely on praying to Allah (SWT) while purging the heart of everything else. The spoken word alone does not convey the oneness of Allah (SWT) (that there is no other deity but He) or the sincerity of religious practice for Him alone. This honesty is a complete lifestyle that encompasses both social and personal life, and it enters the human heart as an idea and a religion.

Sincerity guarantees that worship is focused solely on Allah (SWT), and the Prophet Muhammad (PBUH) throughout his life showed us that deeds are judged only by intentions. Through his blessed life, the Prophet (PBUH) demonstrated that Dhikr is not only a spiritual exercise but also a way to centre the soul, purify the heart, and live mindfully in connection with the Divine.

## Prophetic Examples of Dhikr

The Prophet Muhammad (PBUH) is the epitome of Islamic history, exemplifying the incorporation of remembrance of Allah (SWT) into all aspects of his life. He always starts his day with the remembrance of Allah (SWT). Following his (often lengthy) nocturnal Tahajjud prayers, the Prophet (PBUH) would have a brief slumber before waking up at the call to prayer, Fajr adhan. After completing the sunnah prayers at home, he left for the Fajr prayer. Before attending the congregational fardh prayers at the masjid, he would typically perform the sunnah prayers at home. He and his buddies then remember Allah (SWT) until dawn after Fajr. On occasion, they would congregate near the Prophet (PBUH) and engage in a dynamic, conversational session.

Nowadays, many of us have a habit of checking our phones as soon as we get up, which kills our productivity in the morning. We review our texts, emails, and social media accounts. This has the potential to be quite damaging. Videos featuring scientists and neurologists discussing the impact of this on the brain may be found on YouTube. Your body's natural waking process is disrupted when you check your phone in the morning.

Your brain releases dopamine, a pleasurable neurotransmitter, when you browse through your social media and alerts, which is why it might be difficult to look away from your phone at times. This is also the reason you feel the need to constantly check your phone. In the end, checking your phone first thing in the morning will lead to you lazily wasting your time. And for the remainder of the day, this establishes the pattern.

The first thing you do when you wake up sets the tone for the day. According to a Hadith recounted by Tirmidhi, massage your face and eyes with your palms three times. This straightforward but meaningful act awakens your senses and banishes the grogginess of sleep, enabling you to face the day with consciousness.

After that, give Allah (SWT) your sincere thankfulness for giving you another day. As Muslims, if we take lessons from the life of our Holy Prophet (PBUH), his mornings always began with phrases of gratitude, such as "Alhamdu lillaahil-ladhee 'ahyaanaa ba'da maa 'amaatanaa wa' ilayhin-nushoor" (Praise is to Allah SWT Who gave us life after causing us to die, and unto Him is the resurrection) (Sahih Bukhari).

Each organ has its own kind of worship; Dhikr is how the tongue and heart worship. An ear that does not hear, a hand that does not hold, and an eye that does not see are all analogous to a tongue that does not perform Dhikr. The Messenger of Allah (PBUH) actually asserts that a person who remembers his Lord is alive, whereas a person who does not mention his Lord is dead.

A person is preoccupied with worldly tasks, absent from outward worship, and engaging in incorrect internal worship if they fail to mention their Lord. A person's heart remembers Allah (SWT) even when they are occupied with worldly tasks and perform Dhikr. In actuality, the verse that follows says the following for such individuals:

> *"By men whom neither traffic nor merchandise can divert from the Remembrance of Allah, nor from regular Prayer, nor from the practice of regular Charity: Their (only) fear is for the Day when hearts and eyes will be transformed (in a world wholly new)" (Quran 24:37)*

Additionally, we're commanded to mention and glorify Allah (SWT) often via earnest, terrified, and low-pitched pleading in the chapters of al-A'raf, 7/205, and al-Ahzab. Al-Ankabut chapter 29/45 highlights that the most important act of worship is remembering or mentioning Allah (SWT), which is more important than everything else.

The love of Allah (SWT) and the love of worshipping Him were evident in the Holy Prophet (PBUH) even before he took on the role of Prophet. This is demonstrated by the fact that, although spending his early years in the corrupt and debased society that existed at the time, "Makkah," he never participated in any of the immoral or pointless acts of his fellow residents. He neither ever worshipped an idol nor ate any food offered to it as a sacrifice.

After receiving the call to spread the message of Islam, he demonstrated his love of Allah (SWT) through his devotion to duty in the face of persecution and privations that were bitter, cruel, and sustained. Nothing and no one could affect his high resolve, and no consideration could stand in the way of the performance of his duty. The people of Makkah sought to place all sorts of temptations in his way to persuade him to give up his opposition to idol-worship, but he always proved his love for Allah (SWT) by facing all difficulties bravely.

The Holy Prophet's (PBUH) commitment to and love for Allah (SWT) influenced every facet of his existence. Much of his day and nighttime hours were devoted to worshipping and remembering Him, despite the exceptionally demanding duties that had been placed upon him. At midnight, he would get out of bed and focus on worshipping Allah (SWT), until it was time to leave for the morning prayers at the mosque.

He prayed till his breasts heaved like a boiling pot and his prayer mat got soaked with tears. In the late hours of the night, he would occasionally stand for a very long time in prayer. He did, in fact, demonstrate that he was a devoted, obedient, modest, steadfast, and loving servant of Allah (SWT). In an attempt to have a closer relationship with Allah (SWT), he dedicated every thought, action, and movement of his being to Him.

## Common Dhikr Practices and Supplications (Dua) Used by the Prophet (PBUH)

The Prophet Muhammad (PBUH) regularly engaged in various forms of Dhikr (remembrance of Allah SWT) throughout his life, which served both as a spiritual practice and a source of inner peace. Among the most common and emphasised phrases were "SubhanAllah" (Glory be to Allah SWT), "Alhamdulillah" (All praise is due to Allah SWT), and "Allahu Akbar" (Allah SWT is the Greatest). These were especially recommended after each of the five daily prayers.

In a narration reported in Sahih Muslim, the poor companions came to the Prophet (PBUH), concerned that the wealthy were surpassing them in good deeds due to their ability to give in charity. The Prophet (PBUH) responded by teaching them a powerful form of Dhikr, saying: "Shall I not teach you something by which you will catch up with those who have surpassed you? Say SubhanAllah, Alhamdulillah, and Allahu Akbar 33 times each after every prayer." He also frequently said "La ilaha illallah" (There is no deity worthy of worship except Allah SWT), emphasising its importance in numerous hadiths, such as in Sahih al-Bukhari, where he stated that it is the best form of remembrance.

Furthermore, the Prophet (PBUH) would often say "Astaghfirullah" (I seek forgiveness from Allah SWT), even though he was sinless, as a model for humility and repentance; it is reported in Sahih Muslim that he would seek forgiveness from Allah (SWT) more than seventy times a day. These practices illustrate the central role that constant remembrance of Allah (SWT) had in the Prophet's (PBUH) daily routine, and they offer a timeless model for spiritual mindfulness and devotion.

## Duas of the Prophets

### The Dua of Prophet Adam (AS) – For Forgiveness

> *"Our Lord, we have wronged ourselves, and if You do not forgive us and have mercy upon us, we will surely be among the losers" (Quran 7:23)*

This is the heartfelt plea of Adam (AS) and Hawwa (Eve) after their mistake in Jannah.

The narrative of Adam (AS) includes the first human events and signifies the beginning of all human life. Allah commanded all of His angels to bow down in reverence for Adam (AS), saying, "And [mention] when We said to the angels, "Prostrate before Adam," so they all did, with the exception of Iblees (devil)." He was haughty, refused, and joined the unbelievers. Iblees felt degraded and jealous of Allah's (SWT) most recent creation. Therefore, he resolved to sow discord out of resentment.

> *"I will surely take from among Your servants a specific portion. And I will mislead them, and I will arouse in them [sinful] desires, and I will command them so they will slit the ears of cattle, and I will command them so they will change the creation of Allah." (Quran 4:118-119)*

It is Iblees's mission to create desires in us and give us false hope. He wants to tempt us into believing falsehood, but Allah (SWT) warns us that this is only a deception. Now, at the time, Adam (AS) was in Jannah (paradise) and was given only one instruction from Allah (SWT):

> *"O Adam, dwell, you and your wife, in Paradise and eat therefrom in [ease and] abundance from wherever you will. But do not approach this tree, lest you be among the wrongdoers." (Quran 2:35)*

Adam (AS) was cautioned by Allah (SWT) to avoid the tree in addition to being prohibited from eating the apple.

> *"And Adam and his wife ate of it, and their private parts became apparent to them, and they began to fasten over themselves from the leaves of Paradise," says Allah (SWT), who knows why Adam (AS) fell prey to Iblees's antics and defied Allah's (SWT) instructions. And Adam made a mistake and defied his Lord (Quran 20:120)*

This might be a part of Allah's (SWT) plan to teach us proper behaviour when we make mistakes and disregard our code of conduct. The second thing Adam (AS) did was noble; he immediately accepted responsibility for his conduct and expressed regret for his choice. After being put to the test, Adam (AS) accepted responsibility for his behaviour and asked his creator for forgiveness right away. Adhering to this approach is a clear indication of a Mu'min (believer).

Guilt can really serve as guidance if you pay attention to it; internal issues arise when you ignore or repress the feeling. You can alter at any time; it's never too late. Never give up because you think it's too late for you. Admitting your mistakes and feeling guilty is a wonderful way to show that you believe in and are committed to Allah (SWT) and your faith. We will undoubtedly make a lot of mistakes, but as long as we maintain our faith in Allah (SWT) and keep turning from our sins, we have an opportunity to gain His forgiveness and grow.

**The Dua of Prophet Ayub (AS) – For Relief from Hardship**

> *"Indeed, harm has afflicted me, and You are the Most Merciful of those who show mercy" (Quran 21:83)*

Prophet Ayub (AS) made this dua during his severe trials and suffering, when he lost his health, wealth, and family. His prayer reflects his deep patience and trust in Allah's (SWT) mercy, even in the face of immense hardship. His story teaches us the importance of remaining steadfast and trusting in Allah (SWT) during times of difficulty.

**The Dua of Prophet Muhammad (PBUH) – Protection from Evil**

> *"I seek refuge in the perfect words of Allah from every devil, harmful creature, and every envious eye" (Bukhari)*

This dua is recited to seek protection from all forms of harm, including evil influences, jealousy, and harmful creatures. It is commonly recited for oneself or for children to ensure safety and seek Allah's (SWT) divine protection.

**The Dua of Yunus (AS) – For Desperation and Hope**

> *"There is no deity except You; exalted are You. Indeed, I have been of the wrongdoers" (Quran 21:87)*

This story highlights the powerful dua (supplication) of Prophet Yunus (AS), who called out to Allah (SWT) from the depths of darkness while trapped in the belly of a whale. His words express humility, repentance, and faith. Believers often recite this dua in moments of distress, as it reminds us that turning to Allah (SWT) with sincerity and acknowledging our faults can bring hope and relief, no matter how desperate the situation.

### The Dua of Prophet Musa (AS) – For Confidence and Ease

> *"My Lord, expand for me my breast. Ease my task for me. Untie the knot from my tongue, so they may understand my speech" (Quran 20:25–28)*

Prophet Musa (AS) made this dua before confronting Pharaoh, seeking Allah's (SWT) help for clarity, confidence, and eloquence in his speech. This dua serves as a reminder to ask Allah (SWT) for support when facing challenging tasks, especially when communication and confidence are key.

### Dua of Prophet Ibrahim (AS) – For Righteous Offspring

> *"My Lord, grant me [a child] from among the righteous" (Quran 37:100)*

Prophet Ibrahim (AS) made this heartfelt dua, asking Allah (SWT) for a righteous child. His prayer was answered with the birth of Ismail (AS), a son known for his piety. This dua highlights the importance of seeking Allah's (SWT) help and trusting in His plan.

### Dua of Zakariya (AS) – For Offspring Despite Old Age

> *"My Lord, do not leave me alone [childless], though You are the best of inheritors" (Quran 21:89)*

Prophet Zakariya (AS) made this dua in his old age, asking Allah for a child despite his circumstances. Allah answered his prayer with the birth of Yahya (AS), a righteous son. This dua teaches us to have hope in Allah's (SWT) mercy, regardless of the challenges we face.

**Dua of Prophet Yusuf (AS) – For Steadfastness and Death**

> *"Let me die as one who submits to You and join me with the righteous" (Quran 12:101)*

This dua of Prophet Yusuf (AS) reflects his deep gratitude and unwavering faith after a life filled with trials and triumphs. Despite his high status and success, he humbly asks Allah (SWT) for a righteous end and to be counted among the faithful. It teaches us the importance of remaining steadfast in faith and always seeking a good ending in submission to Allah (SWT).

These authentic and powerful duas reflect the deep sincerity, patience, and trust in Allah (SWT) shown by the Prophet. Muslims are encouraged to learn and recite these prayers in moments of hardship, repentance, hope, and spiritual reflection. Each one serves not only as a plea for help but also as a lesson in faith and submission.

## Adapting Prophetic Practices in Modern Life

These days, people are anxious because life's issues may be seen and felt anywhere, at any time. This is due to both the rapidly evolving technology landscape and the ever-increasing demands of existence. Because of this, people fail to worship Allah (SWT); they are too preoccupied with the world to remember to give life in the afterlife. One of the core precepts of Islam is remembering, which is observed under all circumstances. In every human life, Dhikr is vital. The Quran, hadith, and scholarly agreement serve as the foundation for the sequence of remembering.

The principle of Dhikr is ageless, even though modern procedures may not be the same as those of the seventh century. Despite the loudness, diversions, and technological overload of today's environment, spiritual grounding may be more important than ever. It is possible to develop a spiritual rhythm in day-to-day living by modifying the Prophet's (PBUH) customs to suit contemporary situations.

We must set aside time in our daily routines for performing Dhikr, just as we would for going to the gym or going outside for a walk to unwind. Every day, it could be five minutes after the Fajr prayer or right before bed. We must be committed to it, no matter what it is. The fact that practically every action we perform is accompanied by a prayer is one of the wonderful aspects of being a Muslim. A dua while dressing, a dua when gazing in the mirror, and so forth, we learnt these supplications from Prophet Muhammad (PBUH) as ways to remember Allah (SWT) all the time.

Ordinary actions can become hallowed when Dhikr becomes a way of life. You no longer need to display copies of these prayers throughout your home, thanks to technology. Rather, they are readily available online. It's crucial to keep in mind that forming new habits requires time and work, and that making mistakes from time to time is common. The most essential thing is to keep trying and not give up. Keep in mind that we can overcome these challenges because this is a journey. Make an investment in constancy, or istiqamah. The secret to forming a new habit is to stick with it. Insha'Allah, it eventually becomes a part of your daily routine.

For instance, one can start the day with morning prayers rather than browsing through a phone when they wake up. Moments of silent reflection can be found when walking to class, waiting in traffic, or enjoying a coffee break. Having prayer beads or Dhikr applications on your phone can help you remember important phrases more easily.

Alhamdulillah, after completing a task or a silent Bismillah before beginning work are just two examples of how even fleeting moments can bridge the gap between the sacred and the everyday. The objective is to embody the spirit of the Prophet's life rather than merely copy its form. Muslims can continue to spread the light of his teachings in the modern world by remembering him consciously.

## Creating a Personalised Dhikr Plan Inspired by the Sunnah

Developing a personalised Dhikr plan begins with self-reflection. What moments in your day feel most stressful or quiet? Where can you naturally insert a remembrance without feeling pressured or guilty? Start by selecting a few key prophetic adhkar and integrating them into those moments.

For instance, if mornings are challenging, pick two morning supplications to repeat upon waking. If sleep is restless, recite the Dhikr taught to Fatimah before bed. For emotional healing, adopt *La ilaha illa Anta, Subhanaka, inni kuntu minaz-zalimeen* (There is no deity except You, Glory be to You, I was indeed among the wrongdoers) for personal reflection.

Keep a small notebook or digital journal to track your progress. Note how certain phrases affect your mindset, energy, or peace. Over time, this plan becomes a personal pathway to spiritual intimacy, built on the foundation of the Prophet's wisdom but tailored to your own rhythm and needs.

The Dhikr of the Prophet Muhammad (PBUH) was more than just words—it was a lifestyle of mindfulness, gratitude, and deep faith. In every breath, he turned toward Allah (SWT), showing that the heart's true peace lies in remembrance. By learning from his example, adapting it with sincerity, and creating our own path of remembrance, we can bring that same tranquillity into our lives today.

# Chapter Five

# Developing a Daily Dhikr Routine

## Setting Realistic Goals for Dhikr Practice

When your mind is racing and a storm is raging inside of you, it can seem like there is no way out. Dhikr, or remembering Allah (SWT), is a powerful tool for maintaining composure in happy moments and bringing peace to our most challenging ones. Developing a new habit can be challenging; it can be difficult to go from never making Dhikr to doing so throughout the day.

Making a jump that is too large could demoralise you. Rather, schedule particular times for Dhikr. You can then extend the practice to other times of the day. Everybody has their own daily schedule and routines; fortunately, tying a new habit to an existing one makes it simple to form.

Thus, consider incorporating Dhikr into your everyday activities. Maintaining your focus on God is also made easier when you incorporate Dhikr into an already-existing practice. It's simpler to form habits when you reward yourself. A smart way to start is by setting goals. Establish a reasonable initial objective for yourself.

Reciting 100 Dhikr every day could be your initial objective. Simply establishing a goal increases our likelihood of completing it and is motivating. In any case, goals and rewards are a terrific approach to create enduring, regular behaviours. After you've accomplished your goal, treat yourself to something small. Let's take a closer look at these few ideas for incorporating Dhikr into your daily practice!

## Understand What to Say during Dkihr?

Dhikr can be performed vocally or silently, using different pronunciations of the Thayyibah sentences taught in the Quran or the Prophet's (PBUH) hadith. Reciting Allah's (SWT) names aloud or reflecting on the majesty, glory, and indications of Allah's (SWT) magnificence are two ways to practise Dhikr of the heart. Both are significant (helpful), either as a way to draw nearer to Allah (SWT) or as solutions to different issues encountered, particularly in contemporary society where materialism has a powerful hold. Dhikr phrases come in several varieties. Common examples are:

- **Istighfar**

First, the term *gafara*, which means to close or erase, is the root of the word *istigfar*. Because Allah (SWT) is gaffar, saying Istighfar implies that people beseech Him for protection, to erase their mistakes and shame. Muslims are taught by Islam to constantly increase their istighfar to Allah (SWT).

The purpose of istighfar can be understood as a request for Allah's (SWT) protection so that people can avoid sin, avoid the dangers that come with sin, and ask to be absolved of any minor transgressions. It can also mean a request to be protected so that one does not commit sins again. Additionally, istighfar can provide people with nutrition and alleviate their distress and narrowness.

Secondly, the term *hamd*, meaning to praise or offer praise, is the root of the word *tahmid*. Since the beginning of time, when this planet was brought together for the wealth of divine favours, praising Allah (SWT) has been an act of thanks that combines praise and thankfulness. It is, therefore, natural to begin something with praise and to conclude something with praise. To say *alhamdulillah* is to give thanks to Allah (SWT).

- **Alhamdulillah**

A person who frequently says "Alhamdulillah" will feel as though Allah's grace and love are pouring out on him. If he has a trial, he also says "Alhamdulillah" because he understands that the abundance of blessings is already there and that what he is experiencing is actually a test. So much so that the multiple presents he had already received and benefited from were no longer compared to the ordeal.

- **Tasbih**

Tasbih is a variant of the term *sabbah*, which means "distance," referring to keeping Allah (SWT) away from all bad things, and "running," implying that those who glorify Allah (SWT) do so with greater speed and devotion. Moving away from the edge or initial location is essentially implied by the third definition as well.

According to this interpretation, the individual who swims with his heart in the ocean of Allah's (SWT) strength is the one who glories. The person who glorifies Allah (SWT) can prevent himself from associating Allah (SWT) with others, just as the person who swims can prevent himself from drowning. By uttering Subhanallah, one recognises that Allah (SWT) has no quality or action that is less than ideal, much less repugnant, and that no provision is unjust to all of His creation.

- **Tahlil**

*Al-Ilah*, which implies adoration, is the root of the word *Tahlil*. Allah (SWT) is the one deserving of devotion, the purest love, and exaltation with complete surrender. Thus, if someone says, "Lailaha illalah," he has destroyed all other gods that people worship but Allah (SWT). When someone makes Dhikr, the phrase Lailaha illalah can purge their heart of all the vile thoughts they may have. Furthermore, on the Day of Judgement, someone who consistently and genuinely utters the words Lailaha illalah will receive intercession.

- **Prayer**

The best form of worship that Allah (SWT) has given humanity is prayer. All aspects of a person's being, including their body, heart, and spirit, are used in adoration of Allah (SWT) during prayer. Simply using the body in the ways of standing, kneeling, sitting, and prostration is insufficient to carry out a complete prayer. However, it must be accompanied by both mental and physical emotions.

- **Reciting the Quran**

One way to do Dhikr is to regularly recite the Quran. Those who frequently recite the Quran will reap numerous benefits. Receiving Allah's (SWT) mercy, blessings, serenity, and tranquillity is the primary benefit of regularly reciting the Quran. Reciting the Quran yields the highest reward, with the reciter receiving ten prizes for each letter. Thus, Dhikr can be continued in various ways throughout daily life.

## Balancing Dhikr with Other Daily Obligations and Tasks

Living a whole and spiritually meaningful life as a Muslim requires striking a balance between life and worship. Islam emphasises the importance of keeping a healthy balance between one's spiritual and material responsibilities. In Islam, the idea of worship ('Ibadah) encompasses all facets of a Muslim's everyday life and is not limited to rituals.

By encouraging Muslims to incorporate their faith into everything they do, this all-encompassing strategy makes sure that daily obligations and worship enhance rather than conflict with one another. Many people are curious about how they might fit Dhikr into their hectic schedules while juggling obligations to their families, jobs, and other commitments. Here are a few strategies for effectively earning Dhikr every day:

For Muslims, worship is essential because it gives them a sense of direction and purpose and deepens their relationship with Allah (SWT). Prioritising worship has a positive impact on all facets of life, resulting in a more focused, disciplined, and satisfying life. Islamic teachings place a strong emphasis on striking a balance between one's spiritual and material responsibilities so that neither is overlooked. After every prayer, take at least fifteen minutes to make Dhikr and remember Allah (SWT); however, you are welcome to take more time if you so choose.

Dhikr can be performed orally while doing everyday chores, such as folding clothes, cleaning dishes, or even while commuting to work. Perform Dhikr while working on tasks that require minimal mental focus, such as chores. Additionally, you might develop a checklist for each day of the week and mark out times during the day when you might be able to make Dhikr.

To determine how much Dhikr you have earned this week, you can mark off the times when you have successfully completed it.

> *"The uttering of the words: Subhan'Allah (all glory is due to Allah), Alhamdulillah (all praise is due to Allah), La ilaha illâ Allah (there is no true god except Allah), and Allahu Akbar (Allah is the Greatest) is dearer to me than anything over which the sun rises." (Muslim)*

The numerous difficulties of this worldly existence have rendered it flawed. Allah (SWT) occasionally puts us to the test and occasionally bestows many rewards on us. Insha'Allah, Allah (SWT) will undoubtedly enhance His boundless generosity if we are thankful and remember Him in both good and terrible circumstances. We can also reap the benefits of offering this sincere Dhikr.

## Creating a Structured Dhikr Schedule

Creating a structured Dhikr schedule can help you maintain consistency, deepen your spirituality, and integrate worship seamlessly into daily life. Observing Dhikr at prescribed times enhances its impact, aligns one's actions with divine guidance, and fosters a deep and continuous connection with Allah (SWT). Let's see what specific times are useful to follow:

**Proper Times for Dhikr**

It is crucial to understand when it is appropriate to remember Allah (SWT). One should always be engaged in performing Dhikr.

> *Aishah (RA) says the Holy Prophet used to be occupied in the remembrance of Allah (SWT) at all times (Tirmidhi)*

Nonetheless, the following particular instances are mentioned in the Quran: In other words, keep Allah in mind during "bukra" and "asil." These two periods are extremely important. The term "bukra" in Arabic refers to the time between the sun rising and the first glimmering of light in the sky. In light of this, the meaning would be to perform Dhikr from the time of the Morning Prayer till the sun rises. Thus, this is the first occasion for remembering Allah (SWT), and "asil" is the second. Asil refers to the period between the mandatory "Asr" prayer and the sun's descent. This verse mentions the third, fourth, and fifth times:

> *"So be patient over what they say and exalt [Allah] with praise of your Lord before the rising of the sun and before its setting; and during periods of the night [exalt Him] and at the ends of the day, that you may be satisfied."* (Quran 20:130)

In other words, abide patiently by what these people say, and honour and praise your Lord before the sun rises and sets (both of these times have previously been mentioned); and during the night and on both sides of these, so that your desires may be granted. In addition to the two times already stated, this poem also mentions the time after the sun rises and the early and late hours of the night as being favourable for Dhikr.

The sixth time is the time after every obligatory Prayer. The Holy Prophet, as always, used to continue this Dhikr so much so that it was as if it had become his practice [Sunnah]. Ibn Abbasra relates that, 'When we used to be at some distance we would learn that the Salat had ended upon hearing the Dhikr: The period following each required prayer is the sixth time. The Holy Prophet used to perform this Dhikr so frequently that it seemed to have become second nature to him [Sunnah]. According to Ibn Abbasra, when we were at a distance, we would hear the Dhikr and know that the Salat had ended:

> *"O our Allah! You are the [Embodiment of] Peace, and true peace comes from You. Blessed are You, O Lord of Majesty and Bounty!" (Muslim)*

Additionally, it should be noted that any new activity initially proves to be burdensome, and the heart becomes smaller as a result of performing it. This is why some individuals claim that their hearts are not inclined to conduct Dhikr. However, is it possible to master a new ability in a single day? Of course not! Instead, it takes time for this to become the case and occurs gradually. Therefore, if someone finds it burdensome and their heart is not first oriented towards it, they shouldn't worry. The requirement is that Dhikr must be maintained continuously, but the heart will accept it gradually.

# Chapter Six

# Dhikr and Its Role in Personal Transformation

## Cultivating a Positive Mindset through Dhikr

We frequently adopt either a positive or a negative mindset throughout our lives. A life free from stress and anxiety is possible when one maintains a positive outlook. While negative thinking can be harmful, positive thinking has many advantages. One who cultivates a positive mindset is more likely to treat people with love and respect and to see them in a good light. You will have a good temperament, live a happy life, and have peace of mind and heart if you have a positive outlook.

The mind can be trained to think either positively or negatively. Thought power is a neutral force. Whether the outcomes are favourable and helpful or unfavourable and detrimental depends on how one thinks. The same energy might behave in various ways. Long-term introspection can alter cognitive patterns. To alter your mental attitude, you must be prepared to invest time and effort into avoiding negative thoughts and pursuing positive ones.

Dhikr can be a transformative force, capable of reshaping one's mindset, character, and daily choices. Let's have a look at the profound impact Dhikr can have on personal transformation, exploring how it helps cultivate a positive mindset, instils gratitude, enhances self-discipline, and aids in overcoming personal weaknesses.

The mind is a powerful engine that has the competence to shape our emotions, behaviours, and experiences. However, it is also susceptible to negativity, stress, and hopelessness. Remember that the Shaytan, is eager to mislead the Muslim, deny him good things, and he is the source of evil whispering in the times when we are remembering Allah (SWT). The key to effective remembrance of Allah (SWT) is proper focus, or khushoo'. Making an effort to reflect on your actions and words, considering the significance of the Quran, the Dhikr, and the Dua (supplications) you are reciting, while keeping in mind that you are speaking to Allah (SWT) as though you could see Him. Ihsaan is worshipping Allah (SWT) as though you are seeing him, and when a worshipper stands to pray, he is speaking to his Lord.

In such moments, Dhikr offers a lifeline—a method to centre the heart and refocus the mind on what truly matters. Regular remembrance of Allah (SWT), whether through phrases like SubhanAllah (Glory be to Allah SWT), Alhamdulillah (All praise is due to Allah SWT), or Allahu Akbar (Allah SWT is the Greatest), instils a sense of calm and clarity. When one consistently engages in Dhikr, the act serves as a reminder of divine presence and support. This awareness can neutralise negative thought patterns, such as anxiety, envy, or hopelessness, by replacing them with trust, peace, and optimism. Rather than feeling overwhelmed by worldly challenges, the heart gains tranquillity through a sense of spiritual alignment.

Scientific studies in recent studies have also supported the psychological benefits of repetitive spiritual practices. While Dhikr is much more than a meditative exercise, its rhythmic and focused nature mirrors mindfulness techniques shown to reduce stress and promote emotional well-being. Dhikr, however, goes a step further—it not only calms the mind but also connects the soul to a higher purpose, bringing enduring peace rather than temporary relief.

## Transforming Negative Thoughts and Attitudes with Regular Dhikr

Negative thoughts are not merely fleeting emotions—they can shape identity and behaviour if left unchecked. Jealousy, anger, impatience, and arrogance can become ingrained traits if not consciously addressed. Occasionally, the Shaytan deceives us by claiming that our feelings of sadness or anxiety indicate a lack of faith or that Allah (SWT) is upset with us, but this is untrue. Because everyone experiences sadness and anxiety, which are natural emotions that Allah (SWT) created in us. Sadness and anxiety were experienced even by the Prophets (peace and blessings be upon them all). Allah (SWT) forewarned us that we would be put to the test when we are depressed and under stress, yet He also said:

> *"Allah does not burden a soul more than it can bear"*
> (Quran 2:286)

Individuals do not simply awaken and arrive at such unfavourable conclusions in groups. It begins with a single, fleeting, negative idea that gives rise to an emotion. More negative ideas will follow if you continue to concentrate on that emotion. Every concept begins small, but if you focus on it for a while, you can refine it and make the colours, words, and whole situation more evident.

We refer to this as a negative mental pattern. It entails concentrating on an unpleasant emotion and thinking that it is grounded in reality. Ultimately, you overemphasise both the emotion and the drastic measures taken to address it. This keeps happening until you are certain that your extreme approach is the only viable option.

Through this strategy of negative thinking, Shayṭan may make the most absurd things seem acceptable. We must thus be mindful of our ideas and make a concerted effort to swiftly weed out negative ones. It is far more difficult to resist a notion once you have been thinking about it frequently. Your mind will be able to return to those dark areas more readily because it is aware of their existence.

There is a wealth of material on how to counter negative ideas and have a more positive outlook on life. However, it is crucial to understand that the brain is like a muscle, and strengthening it will take time; you must have patience with yourself. Even though we would all prefer to have a stop button for overanalysing and negative thoughts, there isn't one. However, a healthy routine and plan that includes enhancing mental, physical, and spiritual well-being can significantly lessen these symptoms.

The good news is that we have an easy remedy called Dhikr (remembrance of Allah SWT) that provides an active means of realigning the heart away from these destructive patterns. Consider the practice of repeating Astaghfirullah (I seek forgiveness from Allah). This phrase not only acknowledges one's mistakes but also reinforces humility and accountability. Over time, a person who regularly seeks forgiveness becomes more introspective and mindful of their words and actions. They begin to view life's trials not as punishments but as opportunities for growth and purification. Moreover, when Dhikr becomes habitual, it creates a barrier against the whispers of the ego and Shaytan.

## Building a Mindset of Gratitude and Contentment

Gratitude is a strong inducer of joy and pleasure. One of the most important concepts in a believer's life is gratitude (Shukr). Gratitude is an active, intentional habit that permeates thoughts, deeds, and prayers rather than just being a passive appreciation. Being thankful to Allah (SWT) is a responsibility and a means of spiritual growth.

By expressing our thankfulness, we beg Allah (SWT) to bless us abundantly and cultivate a growing appreciation for His favours. This occurs as a result of our consciousness growing as we walk the road of thankfulness, revealing the many reasons we must be grateful to Allah (SWT). This mutual circle of giving thanks that results in more blessings is exquisitely captured in the following passage:

> *"And [remember] when your Lord proclaimed, 'If you are grateful, I will certainly give you more. But if you are ungrateful, surely My punishment is severe'" (Quran 14:7)*

Dhikr nurtures a grateful heart by directing attention away from what is lacking toward what is already present. It is important to understand that the sincerity and beauty instilled into our memory, rather than the quantity, influence the depth of our thankfulness and connection with Allah (SWT). We can cultivate a deep sense of thankfulness and a closer relationship with Allah (SWT) by making an effort to remember Him with true sincerity, regardless of the amount.

Repeating Alhamdulillah throughout the day—whether after a meal, upon waking, or simply for the ability to breathe—encourages an internal shift. Gratitude becomes less about grand moments and more about consistent recognition of Allah's (SWT) mercy in daily life. This shift transforms how one interacts with the world. A grateful person is less likely to harbour resentment or entitlement and more likely to exhibit patience, generosity, and positivity.

Contentment (qana'ah) also blossoms when gratitude takes root. Through Dhikr, one learns to appreciate Allah's (SWT) decree, understanding that true satisfaction is not found in material abundance but in spiritual richness. This understanding fosters inner peace, even in the face of external challenges.

## Fostering Personal Growth and Character Development

Islam views character (akhlaq) as a fundamental aspect of faith and places a high value on it. Through constant reminders of one's purpose, obligations, and principles, Dhikr plays a vital role in forming and honing character qualities. The Prophet (PBUH) is supposed to have stated that one of his goals was to perfect human morals, or Akhlaq:

> *"I have been sent to perfect the good morals"* (Musnad Ahmad)

The prophetic mission has been to enhance human behaviour with the perfection of moral standards and ethical structures, among other significant things. The Prophet (PBUH) used to make this dua, demonstrating the close and unbreakable bond between Dhikr and Akhlaq:

> *"O Allah! I seek refuge in You from corrupt morals, evil deeds, misguided desires, and chronic diseases"* (Tirmidhi)

A person's heart softens as they perform Dhikr, and their limbs also become more energetic, allowing them to perform any good activity, no matter how difficult it may seem. Neglecting Allah's (SWT) Dhikr causes a person to commit ill deeds. Regular Dhikr connects a person's entire physical and spiritual body to the divine realm, fosters positive emotions, and aids in the management of the soul's bad inclinations (Nafs).

Bad traits, such as pride, false status, arrogance, wrath, envy, and other negative values, are developed when the Dhikr is neglected.

Conversely, a person cultivates good morals and character when he makes Dhikr consistently and truly.

Man is a composite of two elements: "matter" and "spirit". Both of them require their food and supplies. The substance (body) will wither and weaken if its sustenance is interrupted. In a similar vein, the soul weakens if it is not fed or given Dhikr. Additionally, corrupt morals harm the upright moral code by making the weaker soul its victim. Conversely, excessive Dhikr of Allah (SWT) enhances a person's spiritual realm. The Dhikr aids in the development of spiritual awareness and caution, as well as the strengthening of one's faith and heart. Tawhid is a Dhikr that helps believers reaffirm their faith.

Infidelity (kufr) can be transformed into faithfulness (iman) even by Dhikr. Before he converted to Islam, Hazrat Umar (RA) was notorious for his anti-Islamic sentiments. His heart softened, and all of his fury disappeared when he heard some of the Quranic lines. His conversion to Islam brought about a complete change in his thinking, emotions, and consequent behaviour.

Dhikr's influence altered Umar's (RA) life, and his subsequent Akhlaq served as a model for all succeeding generations. A human spirit that avoids Allah's (SWT) Dhikr becomes indifferent to the commandments of Allah (SWT), which eventually leads to the development of undesirable morals in him. However, as we stated in the case of Hazrat Umar (RA), Dhikr has the innate ability to enhance a person's virtues and morals.

## Enhancing Self-Discipline and Moral Character through Dhikr

One of the most transformative aspects of Dhikr is its ability to reinforce self-discipline. Much like physical exercise strengthens the body, spiritual exercises like Dhikr strengthen the soul. When practised with consistency and sincerity, Dhikr becomes a daily anchor that nurtures conscious living.

Self-discipline begins with mindfulness—being aware of thoughts, behaviours, and their consequences. Dhikr acts as a spiritual checkpoint, reminding the believer of Allah's constant presence. This realisation encourages the avoidance of sinful behaviours, not out of fear alone, but from a place of love and reverence.

The famous companion Abdullah ibn Mas'ud once said, "A believer sees his sins as if he were sitting under a mountain which he fears may fall on him." This level of self-awareness is cultivated through regular remembrance, making the heart sensitive to right and wrong. Over time, one develops a strong moral compass, guided not by fleeting emotions but by enduring values reinforced through Dhikr.

## Using Dhikr as a Tool for Overcoming Personal Challenges and Weaknesses

Everyone faces personal struggles—be it emotional wounds, habitual sins, or inner doubts. These weaknesses, if left unaddressed, can become obstacles to growth and fulfilment. Dhikr serves as a spiritual remedy, offering strength to confront and overcome these internal battles.

We occasionally encounter hardships in this world that cause us great emotional distress. These assessments, which are frequently marked by strong feelings, have the potential to develop into actual emotional upheaval. We may become overwhelmed by stress, anxiety, despair, and loneliness, and look for a means to relax. However, Dhikr, or remembering Allah, serves as a comforting salve for our souls during these trying times. Dhikr is more than just a recitation; it is a spiritual remedy that heals us from the inside out, returning us to a state of profound tranquillity and calm.

Words cannot express the tranquillity that Dhikr bestows upon the heart. Consider a youngster who is geographically isolated from their parents. They will experience sadness and dissatisfaction. However, they are overcome with immense excitement as soon as they are once more in their parents' arms. It is comparable to the sense of fulfilment and tranquillity that a disturbed heart feels when it turns to Allah. As though this person were already experiencing the joys of Jannah (heaven), Dhikr turns a troubled heart into a calm one.

In times of distress, a lot of us turn to Allah (SWT). However, persistent practice is where Dhikr's true power lies. Remembering Allah (SWT) is simple when everything is going smoothly, but adhering to it during difficult times is far more difficult. However, this is exactly where Dhikr's beauty resides: it serves as our bulwark during life's turbulence.

By doing Dhikr consistently, we can fortify our patience and trust. Every time we recite Allah's (SWT) name or make an invocation, we are demonstrating our devotion to our faith. Our hearts become more sensitive to the divine presence the longer we continue this exercise. We learn to completely depend on Him, to put His assistance first, and to know that He is always available to lead and console us.

When things are tough, we shouldn't let hopelessness take over. These are the exact times when the great power of Dhikr is shown. It turns inner turmoil into tranquillity, injuries into recovery, and anxieties into faith in Allah (SWT). Dhikr gives us the courage to face hardships with composure and unshakeable faith.

Dhikr is a reminder to the troubled mind and an appeal to the tired spirit. It serves as a reminder that there is a source of serenity that surpasses all obstacles in a world where problems seem to be growing every day. Although we will still confront difficulties, Dhikr provides us with the spiritual resources to deal with them head-on.

When dealing with fear or uncertainty, repeating *Hasbunallahu wa ni'mal wakeel (Allah is sufficient for us and the best disposer of affairs)* can instil courage and reliance on Allah (SWT). When feeling overwhelmed, *La hawla wa la quwwata illa billah (There is no power or might except with Allah)* reminds the believer of the source of all strength.

These phrases are not mere words; they are affirmations of faith that energise the soul. By regularly turning to Dhikr during moments of weakness, a person learns to channel their struggles into opportunities for spiritual elevation. Over time, patterns of self-doubt or sin are replaced with resilience, hope, and unwavering trust in Allah's (SWT) plan.

However, it's crucial to keep in mind that Dhikr shouldn't be saved for times of need. It is a way of life and a practice that ought to be consistent. We develop our relationship with Allah (SWT) and nourish our hearts by reciting His names daily. Thus, Dhikr becomes a source of illumination in our day-to-day existence, a means of elevating our souls and purifying our hearts.

Regular practice turns into a kind of defence against this dunya's challenges and temptations. Thus, Dhikr offers a steady path forward. It is a quiet yet profound companion on the journey of personal growth—one that not only elevates the individual but also brings light to those around them.

# Chapter Seven

# Integrating Dhikr into Different Aspects of Life

Dhikr, the remembrance of Allah (SWT), is not confined to the walls of a mosque or the moments following prayer. As Muslims, we know that it must be a way of life that can be woven into the fabric of our everyday routines. Including it in daily practice and into different aspects of life serves not only to strengthen spiritual awareness but also to bring peace, focus, and purpose to even the most mundane activities. Let's have a look at how Dhikr can be consciously practised during daily tasks, incorporated into work and study breaks, and fostered within the family setting as a unifying spiritual practice.

## Most Famous and Easy Adhkar in Daily Activities

Modern life often pulls people in many directions, from commuting to cleaning, shopping, and running errands. Yet, within these ordinary moments lies an extraordinary opportunity for spiritual connection. Dhikr can be infused into routine activities, transforming them from chores into acts of devotion.

For example, the time spent driving or commuting, which often becomes an occasion for idle thoughts or frustration, can instead be transformed by quietly uttering phrases like SubhanAllah Alhamdulillah, or La ilaha illa Allah. The repetition of these phrases not only engages the tongue but also refocuses the mind, grounding it in gratitude and presence. Even while walking, waiting in line, or doing light exercise, Dhikr can be a companion, keeping the heart engaged with the remembrance of the Divine. A few of the most common and powerful Adhkar to practice in daily life are given below:

**La ilaha illa Allah (There is no god except Allah SWT):**

Saying *la ilaha illa Allah* in this life opens the door to a flurry of good deeds in the next. This little sentence instantly ascends to Allah's (SWT) Throne when spoken. The sins that weigh you down will be lifted on Judgement Day because it will be so weighty. You will have the freedom to enter happiness from any direction, as all eight gates of Heaven will open for you. And you will have achieved your life's ultimate goal if you pass away with the unity of God on your lips.

However, *la ilaha illa Allah* also has positive effects in this world, just like all other types of Dhikr. To defend yourself from the Devil, repeat one variation of the phrase 100 times during the day. Many sins can be pardoned if you repeat them after your post-prayer Dhikr. Knowing that Allah (SWT) is special and that nothing else deserves your undivided devotion is possibly the greatest benefit, even though the person who says *la ilaha illa Allah* is bestowed with many others. Let's have a look at some variations:

- **"La ilaha illa Allahu, wahdah. A'aza jundah, wa nasara 'abdah, wa ghalaba al-ahzab wahdah, fa la shay'a ba'dah"** There is no god but Allah (SWT), alone. He granted His soldiers glory and His servant victory, and He alone triumphed over the factions; there is nothing after Him.

- **"La ilaha illa Allahu, al-'Adheemu al-Haleem. La ilaha illa Allahu rabb al-'arshi al-'adheem. La ilaha illa Allahu rabb as-samawati, wa rabb al-ardi, wa rabb al-'arshi al-kareem"** There is no god except Allah, the Magnificent, the Most Forbearing. There is no god except Allah, the Lord of the magnificent Throne. There is no god except Allah, the Lord of the heavens, the earth, and the venerated Throne.

- **"La ilaha illa Allahu, wahdahu la shareeka lah, lahu al-mulk wa lahu al-hamd, yuhyee wa yumeet, wa huwa hayyun la yamoot, bi-yadihi al-khayru kulluhu, wa huwa 'ala kulli shay'in qadeer"** There is no god but Allah, alone, without partners. His is the dominion. His is the praise. He brings to life and causes death, while He is Ever-Living, never to die. In His Hand is all goodness. He has power over everything.

- **"La ilaha illa anta, subhanaka innee kuntu min adh-dhalimeen"** There is no god except You; all glory belongs to You. I have indeed been among the wrongdoers.

**"SubhanAllah" (All glory belongs to Allah SWT):**

How wonderful God is! The cosmos attests to it, the angels recite it, and the Quran proclaims it. Saying *subhanAllah* means echoing the praise of His Perfection with the rest of creation. This sentence is more important to him than "all that the sun rises upon," according to a hadith from Sahih. The greatest gift is to be alive, see the world, and proclaim the glory of Allah (SWT). Allah (SWT) guarantees us that if we repeat this sentence 100 times a day, either a thousand faults or weaknesses will be removed from our list, or a thousand blessings will be bestowed upon us. There are many variations of SubhanAllah. A few of them are as follows:

- **"SubhanAllahi wa bihamdihi"** All glory belongs to Allah (SWT), and with His praise.

- **"Subhanaka Allahumma rabbi, bika wada'tu janbi wa bika arfa'uh. In amsakta nafsi faghfir laha, wa in arsaltaha fahfadhha bima tahfadhu bihi 'ibadak as-saliheen"** All glory belongs to You, O Allah, my Lord. I lay down on my side by You and I raise it up by You. If You take my soul, then forgive it. If You release it, then guard over it as You guard over Your righteous slaves.

- **"Subhanaka Allahumma rabbana wa bihamdika, Allahumma ighfir lee"** All glory belongs to You, O Allah, our Lord, with Your praise. O Allah, forgive me.

- **"Subhanaka Allahumma wa bihamdika, ashhadu an la ilaha illa anta, astaghfiruka wa atoobu ilayk"** All glory belongs to You, O Allah, our Lord, with Your praise. I testify that there is no god except You. I ask for Your forgiveness, and I turn to You in repentance.

- **"SubhanAllahi wa bihamdihi, subhanAllahi al-'Adheem"** All glory belongs to Allah and with His praise, all glory belongs to Allah, the Magnificent.

- **"Subhana rabbi al-'Adheem, subhana rabbi al-A'la"** All glory belongs to my Lord, the Magnificent. All glory belongs to my Lord, the Most High.

Admiring the beauty of creation is one of the common uses of subhanAllah. Allow the sight of a vibrant sunset to motivate you to glorify God. As you walk through a forest, soar over the heavens, or pause to appreciate a flower along the way, keep this priceless bit of Dhikr on your tongue. You are surrounded by evidence of His perfection and grandeur everywhere you go, so join the rest of creation in praising Allah (SWT) in the morning and at night.

**Allahu Akbar (Allah SWT is the Greatest):**

Allah (SWT) is greater than everything in the world, the universe, and your life. Every time the adhan calls you to prayer, that serves as a reminder, each time you switch places during salah following prayer, and each time you sit for Dhikr. However, remembering Allah's (SWT) greatness is not limited to prayer time. According to Imam Ibn Taymiyyah, takbeer is used to celebrate triumph with the understanding that success comes solely by Allah's power, to humble oneself before His Might, and to ask for strength from Him in trying times.

Do you have any life examples where you might proclaim Allahu Akbar to be a type of Dhikr? The possibilities are infinite. You can say it again when you get good news, during Eid, or when you see an eclipse or other natural miracle. Allahu Akbar will never diminish your triumphs and achievements; rather, they will be magnified with divine grandeur.

- "Allahu Akbar, Allahu Akbar, Allahu Akbar. (Subhana al-ladhee sakhkhara lana hadha wa ma kunna lahu maqrineen wa inna ila rabina la munqaliboon). Allahumma inna nas'aluka fee safarina hadha al-birra wat-taqwa, wa min al-'amali ma tarda. Allahumma hawwin 'alayna safarana hadha watwi 'anna bu'dah. Allahumma anta as-sahibu fis-safari wal-khalifatu fee al-ahl. Allahumma innee a'oodhu bika min wa'tha' as-safar, wa ka'abat al-mandhar, wa soo'a al-munqalabi fee al-mali wal-ahl." Allah is the Greatest, Allah is the Greatest, Allah is the Greatest. Glory be to the One Who has subjected these for us, for we could have never done so on our own. Surely, unto our Lord we are returning. O Allah, we ask You for righteousness and piety in this journey, and for deeds that are pleasing to You. O Allah, make our journey easy for us and shorten its distance. O Allah, You are our companion during travel and the Caretaker of our family. O Allah, I seek refuge in You from the hardships of travel, from witnessing distressful scenes, and from any misfortune affecting our wealth and family.

- "Allahu akbaru kabeera, wal-hamdu lillahi katheera, wa subhanAllahi bukratan wa aseela, Allahu Akbar, wa la na'budu illa Allah, mukhliseena lahu ad-deena wa law kariha al-kafiroon. La ilaha illa Allahu wahdah, sadaqa wa'dah, wa nasara 'abdah, wa hazama al-ahzaba wahdah. La ilaha illa Allahu, wa Allahu Akbar" Allah is the Greatest, and much praise be to Allah, and glorified be Allah at the beginning and end of the day. Allah is the Greatest, and we worship none but Allah, sincerely devoted to Him in our religion, even if the unbelievers hate it. There is no god but

Allah alone, who fulfilled His promise, aided His servant, and who alone defeated the factions. There is no god but Allah, and Allah is the Greatest.

**Alhamdulillah (All praise is for Allah SWT):**

Human beings are naturally drawn to the desire for more. Thankfully, Allah has assured you that there is a path to perpetual growth, and it doesn't call for you to be avaricious, hoard, or overindulge in your quest for more. Gratitude is all that is needed. He says, "If you are grateful, I will surely increase you" (Quran 14:7).

Alhamdulillah, it's easy to practice gratitude and let go of material possessions. Alhamdulillah improves the blessing when you express gratitude for it. Alhamdulillah joins you in your joy when you receive good news. Alhamdulillah makes you appreciate the food He has given you when you consume it. Alhamdulillah helps you maintain perspective during difficult times. At least 100 times a day, at the beginning and end of the day, after sneezing, and after eating, try to recite this Dhikr phrase. Continue to express and feel thankful in any circumstance, and watch as your blessings start to grow. Few variations are;

- **"Alhamdulillahi alladhee hadana lihadha wa ma kunna linahtadee lawla an hadana Allah"** All praise is for Allah, Who guided us to this [rewardable faith and action]. We wouldn't have been guided if not for Allah.

- **"Allahumma ma asbaha bee min ni'matin aw bi-ahadin min khalqika faminka wahdaka la shareeka lak, fa-laka al-hamdu wa laka ash-shukr"** O Allah, every blessing that is received by me or any of Your creation this morning is from You exclusively, so all praise and thanks are for You exclusively.

- **"Alhamdulillahi wahdahu was-salatu was-salamu 'ala man la nabiyya ba'dah"** All praise is for Allah exclusively. Blessings and salutations be upon the one after whom there is no prophet.

- "Ya rabbi laka al-hamdu kama yanbaghee li-jalali wajhika wa li-'adheemi sultanik" O my Lord, to You belongs all praise, befitting the majesty of Your countenance and the greatness of Your sovereignty.

- "Allahumma laka alhamdu anta qayyimu as-samawati wal-ardi wa man feehin. Wa laka alhamdu mulku as-samawati wal-ardi wa man feehin. Wa laka alhamdu anta noor as-samawati wal-ardi wa man feehin. Wa laka alhamdu anta malik as-samawati wal-ardi wa man feehin. Wa laka alhamdu anta al-Haqqu wa wa'duk al-haqq, wa liqa'uka haqq, wa qawluka haqq, wal-jannatu haqq, wa an-naru haqq, wan-nabiyyoona haqq, wa Muhammadun salla Allahu 'alayhi wa sallama haqq, was-sa'atu haqq. Allahumma laka aslamt, wa bika aamant, wa 'alayka tawakalt, wa ilayka anabt, wa bika khasamt, wa ilayka hakamt, faghfir lee ma qaddamt wa ma akhkhart, wa ma asrart wa ma a'lant. Anta al-Muqaddimu wa anta al-Mu'akhkhiru, la ilaha illa ant." O Allah, to You belongs all praise, You are the Sustainer of the heavens, the earth, and whatever is in them. To You belongs all praise, Yours are the dominion of the heavens, the earth, and whatever is in them. To You belongs all praise, You are the Light of the heavens, the earth, and whatever is in them. To You belongs all praise, You are the King of the heavens, the earth, and whatever is in them. To You belongs all praise. You are the Real. Your promise is true. Your meeting is true. Your saying is true. Paradise is true. Hellfire is true. Prophets are true. Muhammad, Allah's blessing and salutations be upon him, is true. The Hour [i.e., Judgment Day] is true. O Allah, to You I submit, in You I believe, on You I rely, to You I turn back, for Your sake I oppose, through You I dispute, it is You I take as a judge. So forgive me for what I did, will do, what I did in secret, and in public. You are The Expediter. You are The Deferrer. There is no god but You.

**La hawla wa la quwwata illa billah (There is no might nor power except with Allah SWT):**

It is certain that you may encounter problems that seem insurmountable or leave you feeling helpless and hopeless. You won't always be able to correct every issue that arises in life, and sometimes that's true. You cannot bring back a cherished departed relative, cure a sick parent, or put an end to a pervasive injustice. However, in times of overwhelm, using this Dhikr word provides perspective and a haven from pain rather than succumbing to despair.

Other than Allah, there is no might or power. Allow these words to strike a chord with you. All power is in the hands of God. If it wasn't written for you, nothing bad can happen to you, and if it was meant for you, then you will gain something from it. Maybe your parents' illness will be a test of patience for you and a way for them to forgive you. Perhaps a more serious injury was avoided by the vehicle accident you had on your way to work. Remember that Allah alone possesses ultimate authority, and try to learn a lesson from everything that happens to you. A few variations are:

- **"La ilaha illa Allahu, wahdahu la shareeka lahu, lahu al-mulku wa lahu al-hamdu, wa huwa 'ala kulli shay'in qadeer. SubhanAllah, alhamdulillah, wa la ilaha illa Allah, wa Allahu Akbar, wa la hawla wala quwwata illa billah"** There is no god but Allah, alone, without partners. His is the dominion. His is the praise. He has power over everything. All glory belongs to Allah, all praise belongs to Allah, there is no god but Allah, and Allah is the Greatest. There is neither might nor power except with Allah.

- **"Masha'Allah la quwwata illa billah"** It is as Allah wills. There is no power except with Allah.

Household chores such as washing dishes, folding laundry, or tidying up can be approached in a similar manner. Rather than viewing these tasks as tedious, they can become moments of reflection. The rhythm of physical movement naturally lends itself to the rhythm of spiritual repetition. Saying Bismillah before beginning a task and Astaghfirullah afterwards embeds mindfulness in every motion, giving each moment spiritual depth.

Additionally, engaging in Dhikr during these times helps counter the feeling of spiritual disconnect that can occur when life gets busy. It provides an accessible way to maintain a connection with Allah (SWT) without needing a specific space or time, making it an ideal practice for those who juggle multiple responsibilities.

## Finding Moments for Dhikr During Work or Study Breaks

The professional and academic environments are often filled with pressure, deadlines, and distractions. These settings can cause mental fatigue, emotional stress, and spiritual neglect. Incorporating Dhikr into brief moments of pause during work or study can serve as a rejuvenating spiritual exercise.

Rather than scrolling through social media or engaging in small talk during a break, spending just a few minutes in Dhikr can recharge both the heart and the mind.

Whispering short phrases such as HasbunAllahu wa ni'mal wakeel (Allah (SWT) is sufficient for us and the best disposer of affairs) or La hawla wa la quwwata illa billah (There is no power or strength except with Allah (SWT) can help ease anxiety and restore focus. These moments, though brief, remind the individual of their reliance on Allah (SWT), promoting a calm and collected mindset.

Moreover, before starting a workday or study session, saying Bismillah invites divine blessing into one's efforts. It shifts the intention from seeking success solely for personal gain to seeking benefit and excellence for the sake of Allah (SWT). At the end of a task, saying

Alhamdulillah offers gratitude for the ability to complete it, regardless of the outcome.

These small acts of remembrance subtly reshape one's professional and academic approach. They help prevent arrogance over achievements and despair in the face of failure, instead instilling a balanced outlook rooted in faith and humility.

## Dhikr and Family Life

One of the most powerful environments for spiritual development is the home. While individuals may engage in personal acts of worship, the collective spiritual life of a household can significantly impact its overall harmony and atmosphere. Encouraging Dhikr within the family setting can nurture a shared sense of peace, unity, and purpose.

Incorporating Dhikr into daily family routines does not require formality. Simple practices, like saying Alhamdulillah together before eating or SubhanAllah (SWT) when observing something beautiful, help build a culture of remembrance. These expressions not only praise Allah (SWT) but also teach children to associate gratitude and wonder with their everyday experiences.

Family members can be encouraged to engage in collective Dhikr, even for a few minutes a day. Sitting together after prayer, during a quiet evening, or while driving, and repeating phrases such as *La ilaha illa Allah* (SWT) or Astaghfirullah as a group fosters spiritual intimacy and connection. It is in these small yet consistent acts that spiritual traditions are preserved and passed down.

Additionally, establishing a routine where each family member shares something they are grateful for, followed by saying Alhamdulillah, can be both bonding and spiritually enriching. This practice reinforces the idea that every blessing, whether big or small, is from Allah (SWT) and deserves recognition.

## Teaching Children and Spouses the Importance and Practice of Dhikr

Instilling the habit of Dhikr in children from a young age lays a foundation for lifelong spiritual awareness. Young minds are impressionable, and when they see their parents actively engaged in Dhikr, it becomes a natural part of their upbringing. More than instruction, children learn through observation. A parent who constantly expresses gratitude, seeks forgiveness, and praises Allah (SWT) in daily speech sets a powerful example.

Teaching children short and age-appropriate phrases of remembrance can be both fun and meaningful. Through repetition, songs, or stories that incorporate Dhikr, children can begin to understand its value. Phrases like Bismillah before eating, Alhamdulillah after sneezing, or Allah (SWT)u Akbar during moments of excitement are simple but impactful ways to introduce remembrance into their lives.

Spouses, too, benefit from mutual encouragement in Dhikr. Rather than making it a solitary pursuit, couples can remind and support one another in remembering Allah (SWT). Whether it's taking a moment for Dhikr together in the morning, sharing spiritual reflections, or listening to the Quran and engaging in remembrance together, these shared practices deepen spiritual connection and marital intimacy.

Sometimes, gentle reminders or leaving notes with Dhikr phrases around the home can inspire reflection throughout the day. For example, placing a card with *La ilaha illa Allah* (SWT) near the entrance or Astaghfirullah in the kitchen can prompt remembrance during transitions and tasks.

By integrating Dhikr into conversations and routines, the entire family learns that spirituality is not limited to prayer or religious study but is part of every moment and interaction. Integrating Dhikr into daily life is a transformative practice that enriches the soul, brings peace to the heart, and aligns everyday experiences with divine purpose. When remembrance of Allah (SWT) becomes embedded in the rhythms of commuting, working, studying, and household tasks, life itself becomes a continuous act of worship. Beyond the individual, cultivating a family environment where Dhikr is shared and encouraged creates a home centred on faith, love, and spiritual connection.

These efforts, though simple, have a profound impact. They teach that spirituality is not separate from life—it is life. Dhikr becomes the thread that ties all moments together, guiding the believer through the joys, challenges, and routines of the world while staying firmly rooted in the presence of the Divine.

## Remembrance of Allah (SWT) through Salat and Quran Recitation

Dhikr, or the remembrance of Allah (SWT), is a fundamental practice in Islam that nourishes the soul and brings a believer closer to their Creator. Among the various forms of Dhikr, Salat (prayer) and Quran recitation are considered the most elevated and complete. These acts combine words, actions, and intentions in a way that fully engages the heart, mind, and body in remembering Allah (SWT).

Salat is the cornerstone of a Muslim's daily worship. It is not just a ritual but a deep, structured form of Dhikr that Allah (SWT) has commanded believers to observe five times a day. The Quran refers to Salat as a means of remembering Allah:

*"Establish prayer for My remembrance." (Quran 20:14)*

Each unit of prayer (rak'ah) involves praising Allah, seeking His guidance, glorifying Him in bowing and prostration, and reciting parts of the Quran. Salat aligns the body and soul in a state of submission, humility, and connection to the Divine.

During Salat, the believer begins by saying "Allahu Akbar" (Allah is the Greatest), entering a sacred space of mindfulness. The recitation of Surah Al-Fatiha, the opening chapter of the Quran, in every unit of prayer is itself a beautiful form of Dhikr, filled with praise, gratitude, and supplication. In addition to the spoken words, the physical movements in Salat—standing, bowing, prostrating, and sitting—symbolise the believer's humility before Allah (SWT), making it a comprehensive act of remembrance.

On the other hand, reciting the Quran is another profound form of Dhikr. The Quran is not merely a book to be read—it is the literal Word of Allah (SWT). Engaging with it through recitation, reflection (tadabbur), and memorisation is an act of worship that fills the heart with light. Allah says in the Quran:

> "And We have certainly made the Quran easy for remembrance, so is there any who will remember?" (Quran 54:17)

Reciting the Quran with sincerity brings peace and tranquillity. It serves as a source of guidance and spiritual healing. The Prophet Muhammad (PBUH) said: "The best of you are those who learn the Quran and teach it" (Bukhari). Both Salah and Quran recitation involve engaging the heart in full awareness of Allah (SWT). They protect the believer from heedlessness (ghaflah), strengthen their faith (iman), and act as a shield against sin.

In essence, Salah and Quran recitation are not merely forms of worship but lifelines for the believer. They are the highest and most beloved forms of Dhikr because they involve a direct, active, and conscious remembrance of Allah (SWT) through His own words and commands. They purify the heart, elevate the soul, and keep the believer rooted in their spiritual purpose.

# Chapter Eight

# The Benefits of Dhikr for Physical Health

## Impact of Dhikr on Physical Well-being

The remembrance of Allah (SWT), or Dhikr, is often seen mainly as a spiritual or religious act. While its spiritual benefits are well-known, there is a growing understanding that Dhikr also plays an important role in supporting physical health. The human body and soul are deeply connected. What benefits the soul often reflects positively on the body. Dhikr, therefore, is not just about saying words—it can help improve overall well-being, including physical wellness.

Scientific research continues to demonstrate the impact of our mental and emotional states on our physical health. Stress, anxiety, and negative thinking are linked to a wide range of health problems, such as high blood pressure, poor sleep, digestive issues, and weakened immune response. On the other hand, feelings of calmness, emotional strength, and mental clarity help improve how the body functions.

When someone engages in Dhikr with sincerity and focus, their breathing becomes slower, their heart rate becomes steady, and their muscles start to relax. These changes are similar to those that occur during meditation and mindfulness practices, which are known to offer numerous health benefits. In this way, Dhikr offers both spiritual peace and physical relaxation.

In addition, Dhikr activates the parasympathetic nervous system—the part of the body responsible for rest and recovery. When this system is active, the body moves away from stress mode and enters a healing state. This helps lower the levels of harmful stress hormones like cortisol and adrenaline. High levels of these hormones over time can lead to inflammation and many chronic health conditions.

By calming the mind and soothing the heart, Dhikr brings peace that supports the body's natural healing abilities. A person who remembers Allah (SWT) regularly may find it easier to handle stress, feel less tired, and manage physical discomfort better. This inner calm creates the ideal environment for the body to repair and maintain its health.

Dhikr is much more than a religious duty—it is a path to overall health. Its power to calm the mind, ease the heart, and relax the body shows just how deeply connected our faith is to our physical well-being. Regular remembrance of Allah (SWT) can be a source of healing and strength for both body and soul.

## Using Dhikr as a Tool for Relaxation and Stress Management

In today's fast-paced digital era, individuals are constantly bombarded by stimuli—from the endless stream of social media notifications to the pressure of meeting personal and professional obligations. This sensory overload, combined with emotional strain and information fatigue, often leads to mental burnout and persistent anxiety. Amid this chaos, many seek peace through various modern wellness techniques, yet often overlook one of the most profound and accessible tools: Dhikr, the remembrance of Allah (SWT).

While Dhikr is deeply rooted in spiritual tradition, its benefits extend well into the realm of mental wellness. More than a devotional act,

Dhikr provides a structured moment of stillness in a noisy world. It cultivates presence. By intentionally repeating sacred phrases with awareness and sincerity, a person interrupts the cycle of scattered thinking and realigns with a state of inner harmony.

Scientific studies on mindfulness have shown how focusing on repetitive phrases or breath helps activate the parasympathetic nervous system—the part of the body responsible for rest and relaxation. Dhikr naturally embodies this principle. When the heart is engaged in the remembrance of Allah (SWT), it sends calming signals to the brain, which can slow the heart rate, reduce cortisol (stress hormone) levels, and even improve digestion and sleep. This biological response is not just psychological comfort; it is physical healing.

Beyond its neurological effects, Dhikr instils a unique sense of spiritual grounding. In modern life, people are often plagued with uncertainty about careers, relationships, or health. This uncertainty breeds anxiety. However, when one consistently engages in Dhikr, it builds a mindset of trust and surrender. Uttering phrases like Hasbunallahu wa ni'mal wakeel (Allah is sufficient for us and He is the best disposer of affairs) instils confidence that even the most troubling situations are under divine control. This spiritual anchoring can serve as a stabiliser when everything else feels uncertain.

Additionally, Dhikr introduces rhythm into a chaotic day. The human body thrives on rhythm—our heartbeats, breathing, and sleep all follow natural cycles. But with erratic schedules, artificial light, and non-stop stimulation, these rhythms are often disrupted. Integrating Dhikr into daily routines—such as during a morning walk, while commuting, or before sleeping—restores a sense of flow. Even a few minutes of repetition can create a "pause" button in an otherwise relentless day, helping individuals transition more smoothly between tasks.

Moreover, Dhikr enhances self-awareness. When one is constantly distracted, it becomes difficult to recognise early signs of stress, such as irritability, fatigue, or shallow breathing. By making Dhikr a habit, a person builds a reflective space to check in with their emotions. It opens a gateway to inner conversations—Why am I feeling tense? What thoughts are overwhelming me? In this way, Dhikr is not only remembrance of Allah (SWT) but also a moment of reconnecting with the self.

For those who experience chronic stress or emotional fatigue, structured forms of Dhikr—such as using prayer beads or counting repetitions—can serve as grounding rituals. These rituals offer predictability and control, especially helpful for those feeling powerless in the face of life's pressures. With time, the heart begins to associate Dhikr with peace, turning it into a safe emotional haven.

In essence, Dhikr offers a simple, cost-free, and profoundly transformative method to combat the mental weight of modern life. It doesn't require silence or isolation. It doesn't depend on ideal conditions. All it needs is presence and intention. In a world where the mind is constantly pulled outward, Dhikr gently calls it inward—toward remembrance, peace, and resilience. Through this practice, stress becomes not just manageable but an invitation to turn toward divine connection and inner strength.

## Dhikr as a Complement to a Healthy Lifestyle

Physical health is best maintained through a balanced combination of nutrition, exercise, sleep, and emotional well-being. Dhikr complements these elements by offering a spiritual foundation that supports and enhances healthy living practices.

When integrated with physical activity, Dhikr can enrich both the exercise experience and its benefits. For example, a brisk morning walk while softly repeating "SubhanAllah" (SWT) or "Alhamdulillah" connects movement with mindfulness. The rhythmic nature of walking aligns naturally with the repetitive rhythm of Dhikr, creating a deeply grounding and harmonious experience. This combination supports cardiovascular health while also cultivating inner peace.

Practising yoga or stretching with a heart centred on remembrance can further deepen relaxation and alignment. Even during gym workouts or jogs, silent Dhikr can be a source of motivation, endurance, and spiritual awareness. The physical act of caring for one's body becomes infused with purpose and gratitude, turning exercise into an act of worship.

Additionally, Dhikr can be used to reinforce positive eating habits. Beginning meals with Bismillah (In the name of Allah (SWT) and ending with Alhamdulillah brings mindfulness and gratitude into eating. This simple habit encourages more conscious eating, reduces overeating, and promotes better digestion.

Sleep, another cornerstone of health, also benefits from Dhikr. Reciting specific supplications or verses of the Quran before bed calms the heart and quiets the mind, making it easier to fall asleep and enjoy a restful night. A relaxed state at bedtime contributes to deeper, more restorative sleep, which is crucial for physical recovery and mental clarity.

Thus, Dhikr seamlessly integrates into all areas of health. Whether moving the body, fueling it with food, or resting it at night, remembrance enhances each action by imbuing it with meaning and intention. It not only supports the body's natural functions but also aligns them with spiritual values.

## Ensuring Balance between Spiritual and Physical Health

In a time where wellness is often compartmentalised—either into physical fitness regimes or spiritual retreats—Islam provides a holistic framework that encourages a balance between the body and the soul. In Islamic tradition, the human being is a complex creation made of both physical form and spiritual essence. The body is not merely a vessel for existence, but a sacred trust (amanah) from Allah (SWT), one that must be maintained with care, responsibility, and gratitude.

Islam does not promote the neglect of either the physical or the spiritual. Instead, it guides believers to integrate both aspects into a meaningful, balanced life. Regular acts of worship like prayer, fasting, and recitation of the Quran nurture the soul. Meanwhile, attention to sleep, food, hygiene, and movement supports the physical body. The practice of Dhikr, or the remembrance of Allah (SWT), uniquely bridges these two worlds, anchoring spiritual mindfulness within the rhythm of daily life and bodily routines.

Dhikr is not limited to spiritual enlightenment—it has profound effects on physical and emotional well-being. When engaged with sincerity and focus, Dhikr has the power to calm the nervous system, reduce blood pressure, and create a sense of inner peace that reflects outward into physical health. The slowing of the breath while repeating the names of Allah (SWT) gently lowers stress hormones in the body. This physiological response, in turn, improves sleep quality, digestion, and even immunity.

Yet, Islam teaches that physical care must go beyond general well-being; it must also be a form of worship. Eating healthily, staying active, and maintaining cleanliness are acts that can be rewarded when done with the right intention. The Prophet Muhammad (PBUH) emphasised the importance of moderation in eating, advised regular movement, and praised strong bodies capable of serving others. In this way, Islam makes the care of the body a spiritual duty, not a worldly indulgence.

On the other side of the spectrum, someone overly focused on physical appearance or fitness without nurturing their inner connection with Allah (SWT) may find themselves spiritually hollow. Temporary satisfaction from physical achievement cannot fill the void left by a neglected soul. Without Dhikr and spiritual reflection, physical health alone cannot bring lasting peace.

True harmony is found when both realms support one another. A spiritually strong person finds motivation to maintain their body because they view it as a gift entrusted to them. Likewise, a physically healthy person finds greater energy, clarity, and presence in their acts of worship. This mutual reinforcement creates a complete lifestyle, one that aligns with the Islamic value of wasatiyyah, or balance.

One of the most significant ways Dhikr supports this balance is by cultivating discipline and mindfulness. Regular remembrance encourages believers to become more aware of their habits. For instance, before eating, saying Bismillah reminds one to consume mindfully. After finishing a workout, saying Alhamdulillah ties physical activity to gratitude. This mindfulness reduces impulsive behaviour, encourages self-control, and promotes intentional living—key ingredients in both health and spirituality.

Moreover, Dhikr anchors the believer during life's ups and downs. Physical health can fluctuate due to illness, ageing, or life's changing circumstances. But the practice of remembrance sustains spiritual health through all seasons. It becomes a steady inner light that supports mental resilience, acceptance, and hope even when the body is weak or in pain.

In essence, Dhikr enhances—not replaces—physical self-care. It magnifies its benefits by embedding spiritual consciousness into everyday actions. Whether one is preparing a meal, taking a walk, or resting, adding remembrance to the moment elevates it from routine to sacred.

In a world that often divides physical wellness from spiritual purpose, Islam reminds us that they are deeply interconnected. Dhikr is the thread that weaves these aspects together. Through it, the body finds stillness, the mind finds focus, and the heart finds peace. This balanced approach to life—where the physical and spiritual walk hand in hand—leads to a life of harmony, gratitude, and holistic well-being.

# Chapter Nine

# Overcoming Challenges in Maintaining a Dhikr Habit

Building a habit of regular Dhikr (remembrance of Allah (SWT) is one of the most powerful ways to bring peace into our lives. However, like any other spiritual practice, staying consistent can be difficult. Life gets busy, the heart feels heavy at times, and distractions can weaken even the best of intentions. Maintaining a steady Dhikr routine and offering practical strategies to overcome them, with the right mindset and tools, we can stay motivated and build a lifelong connection with Dhikr.

## Common Obstacles to Consistent Dhikr Practice

Engaging in Dhikr—the remembrance of Allah (SWT) through spoken or silent praise—is one of the most powerful and accessible spiritual practices in Islam. It connects the heart to its Creator, nurtures inner peace, and strengthens faith. However, for many believers, making Dhikr a consistent habit can be challenging. These challenges aren't just about time management—they involve our thoughts, emotions, environments, and spiritual expectations. Understanding and addressing these challenges is the first step toward a stronger, more lasting connection with Allah (SWT).

## Forgetfulness and Mental Distractions

One of the most common hurdles people face when trying to make Dhikr a habit is simple forgetfulness. Life moves quickly—whether it's work, studies, family, or social commitments, our schedules often leave little room for conscious spiritual reflection, while the flexibility of Dhikr is a blessing (as it can be done at any time), this very flexibility can make it easier to forget. Unlike prayer, which is structured and timed, Dhikr requires more personal initiative. Our minds are frequently full of worries, to-do lists, or distractions from social media and entertainment in that mental clutter, and the act of remembering Allah (SWT) can slip away unnoticed.

## The Perception of "Not Enough Time"

A major misconception that stops people from doing Dhikr regularly is the belief that it requires a special setting—quiet, peaceful, and undisturbed. Many imagine they need to sit in solitude for long periods to truly benefit from it. But in reality, Dhikr is one of the most flexible forms of worship. It can be whispered while driving, walking to class, waiting in line, or even doing household chores. Remembering Allah (SWT) doesn't need a formal setup. Just a few words—like "Alhamdulillah," "SubhanAllah," or "Allahu Akbar"—can be repeated at any moment, and they carry immense spiritual weight.

## Lack of Immediate Spiritual Results

Another challenge is the expectation of instant emotional transformation. Some people try Dhikr for a few days and then stop because they don't feel anything. They expect a spiritual high or a deep sense of peace to wash over them immediately, and when that doesn't happen, they assume they're doing something wrong. But like any practice—physical or spiritual—results come through consistency. Just as exercise strengthens the body over time, Dhikr strengthens the soul through regular practice. It's not about emotional highs; it's about quietly nurturing a connection with Allah (SWT), even when the heart feels distant or dry.

## Feelings of Unworthiness or Guilt

Some people avoid Dhikr because they feel too sinful or unworthy. Thoughts like "I've done too many wrong things" or "I'm not religious enough" create inner blocks. They assume Allah (SWT) won't accept their remembrance because of their past mistakes. But this mindset comes from self-judgment, not divine truth. In fact, Allah (SWT) welcomes every step a believer takes toward Him—especially those who come with broken hearts and sincere repentance. Dhikr is a way to heal, not something that requires perfection before starting. Every "Astaghfirullah" is a step toward mercy. Every "La ilaha illallah" is a door opening to hope.

## Overwhelm from Trying to Do Too Much

Sometimes, in the excitement of becoming more spiritual, people set unrealistic goals. They aim to recite hundreds or thousands of phrases daily, memorise long litanies, or follow advanced routines from day one. While the intention is good, the sudden pressure can lead to burnout. After a few days, they may feel tired, overwhelmed, or guilty for missing their target, and they stop altogether. The key is to start small and build slowly. Even one phrase of remembrance, done consistently and sincerely, is better than a grand effort that can't be sustained.

## Lack of Knowledge or Understanding

When people don't understand the value of Dhikr, they're less likely to prioritise it. They may see it as optional or less important than other acts of worship. But in reality, Dhikr is one of the most beloved actions in the eyes of Allah (SWT). It brings protection from harm, peace to the heart, and light to the soul. The Prophet Muhammad (PBUH) emphasised its importance throughout his life. Gaining knowledge about the rewards and benefits of Dhikr can inspire individuals to incorporate it into their daily lives.

## Environmental and Social Influence

Our surroundings play a big role in shaping our habits. Being in environments where faith is not prioritised can make Dhikr feel out of place or awkward. If you're surrounded by people who rarely talk about spirituality, you may feel shy or hesitant to practice openly. In some cases, people may even mock or misunderstand your efforts. But staying true to your spiritual needs is essential. It helps to find even one or two like-minded friends or join a group (online or offline) that encourages spiritual growth. A supportive environment can make a big difference.

## Negative Internal Dialogue

Another silent barrier is the harsh voice inside some of us. You might think, "I'm not focused enough," "I'm just repeating words," or "This doesn't count." This kind of self-criticism can be discouraging. But it's important to remember that perfection is not required. Allah (SWT) appreciates sincerity, even if the mind wanders. Every time you bring your attention back—even after distractions—you're growing spiritually. Your effort is seen, your intention is valued, and your remembrance is accepted.

## Physical and Mental Exhaustion

Modern life is exhausting. After a full day of work, school, or family responsibilities, many of us are simply too tired to do anything extra. Fatigue can dull our awareness and make Dhikr feel like a burden rather than a relief. Mental exhaustion—from social media, constant news, or emotional stress—also makes it harder to focus. During these times, it's important to remind yourself that Dhikr doesn't need to be long or complex. A short phrase said with love before bed or upon waking can still be deeply meaningful.

## Competing Priorities and Distractions

We live in a noisy world—notifications, emails, messages, and entertainment constantly pull at our attention. These distractions make it difficult to be present in any moment, including during Dhikr. Our attention is divided, and silence feels rare. But even in the middle of the chaos, you can carve out small moments to pause and remember Allah (SWT). Whether it's a few seconds while waiting for your phone to load or during a break at work, those moments matter. Dhikr is not about escaping life—it's about infusing life with remembrance.

Remember, consistency in Dhikr is not about being perfect, achieving spiritual ecstasy, or impressing others. It's about quietly and sincerely remembering the One who created you, who listens to every whisper, and who never leaves you. Every believer faces distractions, fatigue, guilt, or doubts. But recognising these obstacles doesn't mean you've failed—it means you're aware and ready to grow. Allah (SWT) sees every effort, hears every word, and knows your sincerity. Keep going. You are not alone on this path.

## Strategies for Overcoming Procrastination and Distractions

Procrastination and distractions are two of the most common roadblocks on the path to consistent Dhikr. In today's fast-paced, noisy world, maintaining spiritual focus can feel like swimming upstream. We often delay remembering Allah (SWT), waiting for the "perfect moment" or ideal mental state, only to find that such moments rarely come. But the beauty of Dhikr lies in its simplicity, accessibility, and immense reward, no matter how small the effort may seem. Below are mentioned some practical strategies—both traditional and creative—for overcoming the twin challenges of procrastination and distraction, and for developing a sustainable habit of daily Dhikr.

### Start Small and Start Now

The root of procrastination is often perfectionism. Many people feel they have to recite long litanies or reach a spiritual high to make Dhikr "count." But Islam encourages consistency, even in small actions. As the Prophet Muhammad (PBUH) said, "The most beloved deeds to Allah are those that are consistent, even if they are small" (Bukhari). Start with a single phrase like La ilaha illAllah when you wake up. Say it while still in bed before touching your phone. Once this becomes a habit, add SubhanAllah, Alhamdulillah, or Allahu Akbar during different moments of your day. The key is to lower the entry barrier so much that procrastination has no excuse.

### Use Habit Stacking

This technique involves pairing a new habit with an existing one. Because Dhikr is flexible, it pairs easily with daily routines. For example:

- Say *SubhanAllah* while brushing your teeth.
- Say *Allahu Akbar* while locking your door.
- Recite *Astaghfirullah* while waiting for your computer to start.

- Say *La hawla wa la quwwata illa billah* when stuck in traffic.

These small connections create powerful spiritual anchors in your day, turning ordinary moments into sacred ones.

**Create a Dhikr Trigger**

Just like an alarm clock signals you to wake up, create "triggers" that remind you to do Dhikr. Set a daily reminder on your phone titled "Time to Remember Allah." Place sticky notes in common spots like your mirror or laptop that say "Say SubhanAllah." Let these serve as gentle nudges that keep your heart connected throughout the day.

**Design a Dhikr Space**

Your environment affects your behaviour. Designate a small, calm area in your home for quiet remembrance. It can be as simple as a corner with a prayer mat, a Quran, and a tasbih (prayer beads). When you see this space, your mind begins to associate it with spiritual focus. You don't have to spend an hour there—just five minutes a day can help you reset spiritually.

**Use Technology Mindfully**

Technology often distracts us, but it can also assist us. Use Islamic apps that provide daily Dhikr reminders or morning and evening adhkar. Set a phone background with a Dhikr phrase. Listen to soft Quranic recitation or Dhikr playlists while driving or cooking. Instead of letting your phone pull you away from Allah (SWT), let it gently guide you back.

**Replace Idle Time with Dhikr**

We often scroll through our phones or daydream during idle moments. Train yourself to catch these pauses and fill them with remembrance. Waiting for the elevator? Say *Bismillah*. Standing in line? Say *Alhamdulillah*. In these short bursts, you can transform your entire day into a field of barakah (blessing).

## Make Dhikr a Family Practice

Involve your family in remembrance. Recite together after Maghrib, or say *SubhanAllah, Alhamdulillah, Allahu Akbar* as a group before bed. When you turn Dhikr into a shared activity, it becomes more joyful and consistent. Children, especially, will learn the value of spiritual mindfulness from a young age.

## Anchor Dhikr to Salah

One of the most effective ways to stay consistent is to connect Dhikr with your five daily prayers. Make it a habit to recite *Tasbeeh Fatimah* (33 *SubhanAllah*, 33 *Alhamdulillah*, and 34 *Allahu Akbar*) after each prayer, use the peaceful moments after Salah to deepen your connection before rushing back to your day.

## Fight Perfectionism with Forgiveness

Sometimes, we feel like we can't do Dhikr because we're not "spiritual enough" or because we're distracted. But Allah is *Ar-Rahman*, the Most Merciful. He doesn't expect perfection—He values effort. If your mind wanders during Dhikr, gently bring it back without guilt. Even distracted Dhikr carries a reward.

## Track Your Progress

Use a Dhikr journal or habit tracker to see how often you remember Allah (SWT) during the week. This visual reinforcement can be motivating. Don't obsess over numbers—just use them to appreciate your growth and encourage yourself to keep going. Each tick on your tracker is a witness to your love for Allah (SWT).

## Involve Your Senses

Try using a physical tasbih with textured beads to keep your hands engaged while doing Dhikr. Say the words aloud to involve your voice and ears. Write Dhikr phrases in a journal to involve your sight and movement. Engaging your senses helps deepen the experience and improve focus.

**Practice Mindful Breathing with Dhikr**

Try combining deep breathing with remembrance. Inhale slowly and say *SubhanAllah* as you exhale. Repeat with *Alhamdulillah* and *Allahu Akbar*. This method calms the nervous system, improves concentration, and adds a meditative rhythm to your Dhikr.

**Pair Dhikr with Gratitude**

Start your Dhikr session by thinking of one blessing you're grateful for. Then say *Alhamdulillah*. This reflection strengthens your emotional connection to the words you're reciting, making them more meaningful and heartfelt.

**Reward Yourself**

Positive reinforcement works. Give yourself a small reward when you meet your Dhikr goals—a favourite snack, extra relaxation time, or a peaceful walk. Associating remembrance with positivity helps anchor the habit emotionally.

**Seek Spiritual Companionship**

Surround yourself with people who also value Dhikr. Join an online or local halaqah (study circle) where you discuss spiritual habits. When others are striving toward Allah (SWT), it becomes easier and more natural for you to do the same.

Procrastination and distractions may never fully disappear, but you can learn to manage and rise above them. Dhikr is a gentle practice that fits into even the busiest of lives. You don't need the perfect mood, place, or mindset to begin—just a sincere heart and a willingness to remember. Every step you take toward Allah (SWT), He takes many more toward you. Let Dhikr become your anchor, your sanctuary, and your path to peace—one breath, one phrase, one moment at a time.

## Maintaining Motivation and Consistency

Staying motivated requires both intention and inspiration. Begin by reminding yourself why you want to build this habit. Is it to feel closer to Allah (SWT)? To calm your heart? To gain reward for the Hereafter? Keep that goal in front of you, and let it drive your effort.

Be patient with yourself. Habits take time to develop. If you miss a day, don't give up. Instead, gently bring yourself back the next day. Remember, Allah (SWT) loves consistency, even if the action is small. Avoid comparing yourself to others. Your journey is unique. Some people may do more Dhikr, and some may do less. What matters is your sincerity and your effort. Celebrate your own progress, even if it feels small.

You can also stay inspired by reading about the rewards of Dhikr. Knowing that every SubhanAllah (SWT) is a tree planted in Jannah or that remembering Allah (SWT) brings you peace like nothing else can—it motivates the heart to continue, even on tough days.

### Setting Achievable Milestones and Celebrating Progress

Breaking your Dhikr goals into smaller steps makes the process manageable. Instead of aiming to remember Allah (SWT) all day long from the start, set simple milestones. For example:

- Week 1: Say SubhanAllah (SWT) 33 times after Fajr.
- Week 2: Add Alhamdulillah 33 times after Maghrib.
- Week 3: Introduce a morning La ilaha illAllah (SWT) routine.

Each week, add just one more action. Over time, these small steps grow into a powerful, life-changing habit. Celebrate these achievements. You don't need a big reward—just acknowledging your progress is enough. Say Alhamdulillah for the effort. Share your journey with a friend or journal your experience. This strengthens your commitment.

## Seeking Support from the Community and Using Motivational Tools

Developing the habit of regular Dhikr, or the remembrance of Allah, is a journey that becomes much more fulfilling and sustainable when we do not travel it alone. Human beings are social creatures, and having a support system can make a tremendous difference in staying consistent and motivated. Whether it's a friend, a relative, or someone from your local community, involving others in your spiritual journey can bring encouragement, accountability, and joy to the process.

Start by reaching out to someone you trust who also wishes to grow closer to Allah. It could be a sibling, a cousin, or a fellow member of your masjid. Set a time once a week to check in with each other. Use that time to discuss your progress, share what methods helped you stay on track, and talk about any difficulties you encountered. This kind of mutual support builds consistency and reminds you that you're not alone in striving to become more mindful of Allah in your daily life.

Another helpful step is connecting with a community that shares your goal. This can be as simple as attending regular study circles or short reminders offered at your local masjid. The benefit of such gatherings is immense. When you're in a space where the remembrance of Allah is frequent and sincere, it uplifts your heart and makes you feel spiritually nourished. Witnessing others engaged in Dhikr can also motivate you to do more and push through moments of spiritual laziness or distraction.

If attending in-person events is not always feasible, consider joining online forums or groups focused on Islamic learning and practice. Social media can be a valuable resource if used wisely. Following respected scholars or motivational Islamic content creators can keep you reminded of your goals and offer practical tips for staying on

# HABITUAL PEACE

course. Many scholars share brief yet impactful reflections that can be the boost you need on a busy day to bring your heart back to Allah (SWT).

In addition to community support, using motivational tools can greatly aid your progress. The modern world offers numerous digital aids specifically designed for those seeking to deepen their connection with Dhikr. For instance, Dhikr mobile applications come with features like daily reminders, counter tools, and even motivational quotes from the Quran or Hadith. These apps serve as a gentle nudge throughout your day, reminding you to take a moment and engage in remembrance.

Digital tasbeeh counters are another great tool. Lightweight and easy to use, these devices make it simple to keep track of your recitations. They're especially useful when you're commuting, waiting in line, or simply sitting in a quiet moment. Just having one in your pocket or on your wrist can prompt you to take advantage of otherwise idle time for spiritual gain.

For those who prefer physical tools, printable Dhikr cards are a lovely option. These small cards can be placed in places you frequent, like your desk, kitchen counter, or near your prayer mat. Seeing reminders with phrases like *SubhanAllah*, *Alhamdulillah*, or *La ilaha illallah* can gently steer your heart back to the remembrance of your Creator.

Another uplifting method is listening to audio content that centres on Dhikr. You might find nasheeds or spoken-word reminders especially helpful during parts of the day when speaking aloud isn't practical—like when you're working, exercising, or feeling too tired to actively recite. Letting these peaceful, spiritual sounds fill your environment can create a calm and reflective atmosphere that naturally encourages inward remembrance.

The beauty of Dhikr is that it can be practised in many ways, and everyone can find a method that suits their lifestyle. What matters most is consistency, sincerity, and the intention to grow closer to Allah

(SWT). Whether you're whispering His name on your morning walk, joining a weekly group of fellow believers, or using a digital counter in your downtime, each effort is valuable and seen by Allah (SWT).

Remember, building a habit of Dhikr isn't about perfection; it's about progress. Having the support of others and using tools that simplify the journey can transform what may seem like a difficult task into something achievable and deeply rewarding. Stay connected, stay inspired, and keep your heart anchored in the remembrance of your Lord.

# Chapter Ten

# The Impact of Dhikr on the Akhirah (Hereafter)

This life is temporary, and everything in it—our joys, hardships, and struggles—will eventually come to an end. What remains are our deeds, our intentions, and how close we remained to Allah (SWT). Among the most powerful and easiest acts that prepare a believer for the Hereafter is Dhikr—the remembrance of Allah (SWT). While Dhikr brings peace and blessings in this world, its true and lasting rewards are found in the next life. In this chapter, we examine how Dhikr aids in preparing for the Hereafter, the spiritual benefits it provides beyond this world, and its crucial role in our journey toward eternal peace.

## Spiritual Rewards and Benefits in the Akhirah

The rewards of Dhikr in the Akhirah (Hereafter) are beyond imagination. Every word of remembrance spoken sincerely earns a place for us in the next life. The Prophet Muhammad (PBUH) said,

> "Shall I not inform you of the best of your deeds, the purest of them with your Master, and the one which raises you most in rank?" They said, "Yes, O Messenger

of Allah (SWT)!" He said, "The remembrance of Allah (SWT) (Dhikr)." (Tirmidhi)

Every SubhanAllah (Glory be to Allah (SWT), Alhamdulillah (All praise is due to Allah (SWT), and Allahu Akbar (Allah (SWT) is the Greatest) carries rewards that are multiplied many times over. In another Hadith, the Prophet (PBUH) said,

> "Whoever says 'SubhanAllah (SWT)i wa bihamdihi' (Glory is to Allah (SWT) and praise is to Him) one hundred times a day, his sins will be forgiven even if they were as much as the foam of the sea." (Bukhari)

These promises are not just comforting—they are a reminder that Allah (SWT) values the efforts of His servants, no matter how small. In the Akhirah, when we will desperately need good deeds on our scale, these simple acts of Dhikr can be what saves us. They don't require wealth, strength, or special knowledge. All they require is a heart that remembers and a tongue that speaks.

## Quranic Promises and Hadith About the Rewards of Dhikr in the Hereafter

The Quran is full of verses that speak of the reward awaiting those who remember Allah (SWT) frequently. Allah (SWT) says:

> "...the men who remember Allah (SWT) often and the women who do so–for them Allah (SWT) has prepared forgiveness and a great reward." (Quran 33:35)

This "great reward" includes entry into Paradise, peace on the Day of Judgment, and being close to Allah (SWT) in the Hereafter. The

Prophet (PBUH) mentioned that among the people of Paradise, those who remembered Allah (SWT) often will have the highest ranks.

> *"The Mufarridun have gone ahead." The Companions asked, "Who are the Mufarridun, O Messenger of Allah (SWT)?" He said, "Those who remember Allah (SWT) often, men and women." (Muslim)*

From this, we learn that Dhikr is not a small practice with small outcomes—it is a pathway to Allah (SWT)'s pleasure, forgiveness, and closeness. On the Day of Judgment, when many will be in fear and distress, those who spent their time remembering Allah (SWT) will be safe and elevated.

## Understanding the Significance of Dhikr for Salvation and Eternal Peace

When we think about salvation, we often focus on avoiding sin or fulfilling major obligations like prayer and fasting. While those are essential pillars of our faith, Dhikr is the soft thread that ties the heart to Allah (SWT) in every moment. It strengthens faith, deepens love for the Creator, and keeps our focus on what truly matters—the Akhirah.

Dhikr acts as a purifier of the heart. A clean, sincere heart is the foundation of salvation.

> *"The Day when neither wealth nor children will benefit [anyone], except one who comes to Allah (SWT) with a sound heart." (Quran 26:88-89)*

Through constant remembrance, the heart becomes soft and alert. It is more likely to repent, to be humble, and to seek truth. These qualities are signs of a heart ready for the Hereafter. A person who dies while remembering Allah (SWT), or with the name of Allah (SWT) on their tongue, is promised a beautiful end and a blessed return.

## Preparing for the Akhirah through Daily Dhikr

The best way to prepare for life after death is to build daily habits that keep us connected to Allah (SWT). Dhikr is like planting seeds in the soil of our soul. With each repetition of *SubhanAllah* (SWT), *Alhamdulillah*, or *La ilaha illAllah* (SWT), we nurture our faith and water the roots of our relationship with Allah (SWT).

Making Dhikr a part of our everyday life—during quiet moments, after prayer, or while doing chores—trains us to think beyond this world. We become aware that our time is short and our true home is not here. This awareness helps us live more purposefully, make better choices, and turn to Allah (SWT) more often. Daily Dhikr is also a form of protection. It shields us from despair, arrogance, and heedlessness. It keeps the memory of the Akhirah fresh in our hearts. When the thought of death does not scare but instead motivates us to do good, we know we are on the right path.

**Using Dhikr to Strengthen Faith and Readiness for the Hereafter**

Faith (iman) is a dynamic, living entity—it's not something that can simply be switched on and off. Just as a flame requires fuel to stay alight, our faith needs continuous nurturing to thrive. Without the right nourishment, our connection with Allah (SWT) can weaken, and we may drift away from the path of righteousness. Among the most powerful tools to strengthen and sustain our faith is Dhikr, the remembrance of Allah. Through Dhikr, we build a stronger relationship with our Creator, cultivate gratitude, and prepare ourselves for the challenges of life and the certainty of the Hereafter.

Dhikr acts as a vital fuel for our faith. Repeating words of remembrance, such as "SubhanAllah" (Glory be to Allah), "Alhamdulillah" (All praise is due to Allah), and "Allahu Akbar" (Allah is the Greatest), brings us into a state of constant awareness of Allah's presence. This regular remembrance keeps us spiritually nourished, helping to guard against distractions that pull us toward worldly concerns. With each repetition of these sacred phrases, our hearts are reminded of the eternal truths that transcend the fleeting nature of this life. Our attachment to the material world, with all its promises of comfort and satisfaction, begins to loosen as we are drawn closer to what truly matters—the worship of Allah (SWT) and the anticipation of the Akhirah, the Hereafter.

One of the most profound effects of Dhikr is its ability to bring peace to the soul. Life's trials and tribulations can often leave us feeling anxious, stressed, or uncertain. In those moments, Dhikr provides a calming refuge. By remembering Allah (SWT), we are reminded that He is always with us, guiding, supporting, and protecting us. This assurance fosters a deep sense of tranquillity in our hearts, as we trust in the wisdom of Allah's plan. The more we engage in Dhikr, the more we develop a peaceful and grounded outlook on life, regardless of the challenges we may face.

Another significant benefit of Dhikr is that it helps prepare us for the inevitable trials of life. As we repeat the names of Allah (SWT), we begin to shift our focus away from worldly fears and anxieties. The temporary struggles we face no longer seem as overwhelming when we remember that they are part of a larger, divine plan. Dhikr teaches us patience in times of difficulty, reminding us that Allah (SWT) is the ultimate source of strength. By turning to Him in moments of hardship, we can develop resilience and perseverance, ready to face any challenges that come our way with faith and hope.

Furthermore, Dhikr increases our readiness for the Hereafter. The Prophet Muhammad (PBUH) taught us that, "Whoever loves to meet Allah (SWT), Allah (SWT) loves to meet him" (Bukhari). This powerful hadith highlights the deep connection between Dhikr and our readiness for the Afterlife. When we engage in Dhikr, we are developing a love for Allah (SWT) and, in turn, preparing ourselves to meet Him on the Day of Judgment. The more we remember Allah (SWT) in this life, the more our hearts long for the eternal reward that awaits us. Through Dhikr, we can detach ourselves from worldly attachments and approach the Hereafter with calmness and confidence, knowing that our efforts have drawn us closer to the Divine.

Dhikr also serves as a reminder of the ultimate goal in life: to achieve closeness to Allah and secure a place in Paradise. The more we remember Allah, the more we align our hearts and actions with His will. This constant remembrance helps us to stay focused on our ultimate purpose, helping us make choices that are pleasing to Him. It softens our hearts, making us more compassionate, humble, and aware of the needs of others. As we engage in Dhikr, we begin to embody the qualities of a true believer, striving for righteousness and sincerity in all that we do.

Dhikr is not just an act of worship; it is a transformative practice that strengthens our faith, increases our awareness of Allah's presence, and prepares us for the challenges of this world and the Hereafter. Through regular remembrance, we develop patience, resilience, and a sense of tranquility, helping us navigate life's trials with grace. As we draw closer to Allah (SWT) through Dhikr, we also become more ready to meet Him in the Hereafter, where our efforts will be rewarded with eternal success. By making Dhikr a part of our daily lives, we ensure that our faith remains strong, our hearts remain peaceful, and our readiness for the Hereafter is secure.

## Reflecting on the Purpose and Impact of Dhikr in Achieving Eternal Success

In the journey of life, it's easy to become consumed by worldly goals—career achievements, wealth, recognition, or material comfort. While these things may bring temporary satisfaction, they are not the true measure of success in the eyes of Allah (SWT). When we step back and reflect, we begin to understand that Dhikr—the remembrance of Allah—is not just a spiritual exercise; it is a path to eternal success. It's a means to prepare the soul for what comes after this temporary world comes to an end.

So, why do we engage in Dhikr? Is it simply to calm the heart or to fulfil a religious duty? Or does it serve a far greater purpose that stretches beyond this life? The answer lies in the depth of Dhikr's impact on the soul. Every time we remember Allah (SWT), whether by uttering His names, reciting Quranic verses, or simply reflecting on His mercy and greatness, we are polishing our hearts and preparing our souls for the ultimate meeting—with our Creator.

True success is not found in how much we accumulate, how many degrees we earn, or how popular we become. The real victory lies in arriving before Allah (SWT) with a heart full of faith, sincerity, and devotion. Dhikr helps us reach that state by anchoring us in remembrance during both moments of ease and times of hardship. When life is smooth, it reminds us not to forget the One who made it so. When we struggle, it gives us strength and peace by reconnecting us to the One who controls all outcomes.

Each act of Dhikr, no matter how small it may seem, holds deep spiritual value. The Prophet Muhammad (PBUH) reminded us that the tongue moistened with remembrance is beloved to Allah. When we say *SubhanAllah* (Glory be to Allah), *Alhamdulillah* (All praise is due to Allah), or *Allahu Akbar* (Allah is the Greatest), these words are not empty sounds. They are written by the angels, recorded in our book of deeds, and will testify for us when nothing else can speak.

Think of Dhikr as a kind of spiritual investment. Just as we save money for the future, we are also depositing rewards for the Hereafter every time we remember Allah (SWT). These moments of remembrance will shine as lights in our graves, which are otherwise described as dark and lonely places. They will act as a shield on the Day of Judgment, when the sun will be close and people will be desperate for any shade. Dhikr will stand as evidence of our connection to Allah (SWT) and will draw us closer to Paradise, step by step.

It's important to realise that the impact of Dhikr is not limited to the future; it also transforms our present. The heart that regularly engages in remembrance becomes softer, more peaceful, and less attached to worldly distractions. A person who remembers Allah (SWT) will often naturally make better choices, speak more kindly, and react with greater patience. This internal change is a sign that Dhikr is working on the soul, quietly but powerfully.

Moreover, Dhikr has a unique way of filling the spiritual void that so many people experience. Even those who have everything in life—wealth, beauty, status—often feel a sense of emptiness. This is because the soul was created to be nourished by something more than the material world. It was created to connect with its Lord. Dhikr fulfils that need. It reminds us that we are not alone, that our Creator loves us, and that our lives have purpose beyond the surface-level pursuits of this world.

We should also remember that Dhikr is not restricted to specific moments or rituals. It can be done at any time—while walking, cooking, commuting, or lying in bed. Its simplicity is part of its beauty. Even just repeating "*Astaghfirullah*" (I seek forgiveness from Allah) after a mistake can elevate your heart and bring you back to the right path. These seemingly small actions are often the ones that weigh heavily on the scales of the Hereafter.

In the end, the purpose of Dhikr is to cultivate a life that is God-centered, a heart that is at peace, and a soul that is ready to meet its Creator. It is a companion that never abandons us—not in life, not in death, and not in the afterlife. By engaging in Dhikr regularly and sincerely, we pave the way toward real, everlasting success—one that is measured not by fleeting gains but by the closeness we achieve with Allah (SWT).

## The Spiritual Significance of "Hu" in Dhikr and Tawhid

In Islamic spirituality, particularly within Sufi tradition, the invocation of "Hu" carries profound significance. Though it translates simply to "He" in Arabic, its use in Dhikr (remembrance of God) transcends basic linguistic meaning. This sacred utterance serves as a key to unlocking a deeper awareness of tawhid (the absolute oneness of God) and the path to ma'rifah (inner spiritual knowledge). "Hu" becomes a direct reference to God's essence, bypassing attributes or requests, and symbolising a connection with the Divine that is pure, sincere, and stripped of material intention.

### "Hu" as the Heart of Spiritual Remembrance

Unlike many divine names that describe specific attributes of God—such as "Ar-Rahman" (The Merciful) or "Al-Hakim" (The Wise)—the use of "Hu" does not describe a particular trait. Instead, it refers to God's very being. For many spiritual seekers, this simplicity is not a limitation but rather a profound strength. Saying "Hu" in Dhikr is a direct acknowledgement of the existence of God without intermediary concepts. It expresses a state of presence with the Divine, one that does not rely on elaborate praise or supplication.

Islamic scholars have long acknowledged the weight of this Dhikr. It's not just a vocal practice but a meditative state, one that aligns the soul with the fundamental truth that only God truly exists, while everything else is transient and dependent upon Him.

### Understanding "Hu" as a Symbol of Divine Existence

Prominent thinkers like Al-Tirmidhi and Al-Nabulsi have explored "Hu" as more than a pronoun. They view it as a symbolic representation of Divine Reality—one that cannot be fully comprehended by the human mind. Al-Tirmidhi emphasised that all other divine names and attributes stem from the essence that "Hu" points to. This makes it a focal point for the heart in its search for God.

Al-Nabulsi added further insight by explaining that even the act of saying "Hu" implies a level of existence shared with the Divine—not as equals, but as dependent beings. For a person to be able to say "Hu" they must be given existence by God. Thus, reciting this word is itself a spiritual moment, reflecting God's will and sustaining power.

**The Psychology of Focusing on "Hu"**

Classical scholar Al-Razi noted that the human mind cannot attend to multiple things at once. When someone engages in the Dhikr of "Hu" they are directing their full mental and emotional energy toward God. This singular focus helps silence worldly thoughts and distractions. It becomes a moment of true spiritual clarity where only God occupies the believer's consciousness.

Unlike other phrases that may carry implied requests or hopes—such as invoking God's mercy or provision—saying "Hu" is not connected to any material desire. It is simply a pure acknowledgement of God's presence. That alone makes it a powerful expression of ikhlas (sincerity).

**"Hu" and Pure Devotion**

One of the most distinctive features of the "Hu" Dhikr is that it is free from supplication. It is not a call for help, guidance, or blessings—it is simply a declaration of Divine Existence. This reflects a profound level of trust in God's wisdom and generosity.

A hadith qudsi conveys that those who remember God without asking for anything are still granted the best of what others request. This points to a special status of such worship, where the act of remembrance itself becomes a form of complete reliance and surrender.

In such remembrance, the believer is saying, in essence: "I do not need to ask, for I know You already know my needs better than I do."

## A Path for the Spiritually Advanced

Within Sufi teachings, "Hu" is considered a form of Dhikr practised by the spiritually elite, known as khawass. These individuals are not concerned with verbal complexity or ritualistic repetition. For them, a single utterance of "Hu" encompasses all meanings, all prayers, and all worship. It reflects an inner state of constant awareness of God. They do not need reasons to remember God—they live in that remembrance.

This aligns with the concept of muraqabah, or constant spiritual vigilance, where the heart is always aware of God's presence. In this elevated state, the Dhikr of "Hu" becomes an ongoing, silent affirmation of divine reality that saturates every moment of life.

## Realisation of Oneness Through "Hu"

The phrase *"La ilaha illa Hu"* (There is no deity except He) signifies a refined form of monotheism. It emphasises not just that God is the only one to be worshipped, but that He alone truly exists. Everything else is a creation, temporary and sustained by God's will. This view leads to a realisation where the heart recognises no power, permanence, or reality apart from God.

> *"Everything will perish except His Face." (Quran 28:88)*

For those on the spiritual path, this verse affirms that only Allah remains when all else fades. The Dhikr of "Hu" aligns with this truth by focusing solely on the Eternal, the One beyond time and space.

Engaging regularly in the remembrance of "Hu" has tangible effects on a believer's life. It fosters inner peace, detachment from worldly anxieties, and a consistent sense of divine presence. It leads to better behaviour, more compassion, and a life lived in harmony with God's will. This form of remembrance grounds the soul in contentment and submission, knowing that everything happens through Divine decree. Even life's hardships are understood as part of a larger, divine wisdom. This gives the believer strength, patience, and resilience.

The spiritual practice of invoking "Hu" is much more than a vocal utterance—it is a profound expression of faith, trust, and unity with God. It reflects the ultimate level of sincerity, where remembrance is done not for reward or response, but out of pure devotion.

By internalising the message of "Hu" the believer comes to realise that God is all there is, and everything else is merely passing. This realisation brings one closer to the essence of tawhid, transforms the heart, and opens the door to ma'rifah—the intimate, experiential knowledge of the Divine. In the stillness of that one syllable—"Hu"—lies the entire universe of spiritual truth.

# Chapter Eleven

# Embracing Dhikr as a Lifelong Practice

Dhikr, the remembrance of Allah (SWT), is more than just a daily act—it is a lifelong journey that enriches the soul and draws us closer to our Creator. Throughout this book, we've explored how Dhikr strengthens faith, brings peace, protects the heart, and prepares us for the Hereafter. In this final chapter, we will reflect on the major lessons we've learned, understand how to turn Dhikr into a consistent habit, and gain inspiration from the stories of those who have embraced this beautiful practice for life.

## Summary of Key Takeaways and Benefits

Dhikr is a simple yet powerful form of worship that can be practised at any time, anywhere. Its blessings are both immediate and eternal. Spiritually, Dhikr helps us remember our purpose and maintain a connection with Allah (SWT). It keeps our hearts alive and soft, increasing our love for Allah (SWT) and our awareness of His presence.

Emotionally, Dhikr calms the mind and soothes the soul. Saying phrases like SubhanAllah (SWT) (Glory be to Allah (SWT), Alhamdulillah (All praise is due to Allah (SWT), and La ilaha illAllah (SWT) (There is no Allah (SWT) but Allah (SWT) brings inner peace. These phrases remind us that we are never alone and that Allah (SWT) is always near.

Physically, while Dhikr doesn't involve movement like prayer or fasting, it can still impact the body. A peaceful mind leads to better health, reduced stress, and improved sleep. Many people find that making Dhikr regularly helps them deal with anxiety, fear, or loneliness.

Perhaps one of the most important takeaways is that Dhikr is accessible to everyone. It doesn't require wealth, education, or physical strength. Whether you're a student, parent, worker, or elder, you can engage in the remembrance of Allah (SWT) and enjoy its blessings every day.

## Recap of the Spiritual, Emotional, and Physical Benefits of Dhikr

Let's briefly revisit some of the key benefits of Dhikr. Dhikr, the remembrance of Allah (SWT), offers numerous benefits that span spiritual, emotional, and physical dimensions. Spiritually, engaging in Dhikr draws one closer to Allah, helping to deepen the connection with the Creator. This practice purifies the heart and strengthens faith, or iman, fostering a sense of spiritual clarity and devotion. Additionally, regular Dhikr invites forgiveness and divine mercy, reminding believers of Allah's grace and offering a path to spiritual healing and renewal.

Emotionally, Dhikr plays a powerful role in providing comfort during challenging times. Whether facing stress, sadness, or uncertainty, the repetition of Allah's name serves as a source of solace and reassurance. It calms the mind, creating a peaceful space amidst life's turbulence. Dhikr also builds important emotional qualities such as patience and gratitude, two virtues that help one cope with life's difficulties. As practitioners increase their mindfulness through Dhikr, they often experience a profound sense of inner calm, cultivating a peaceful emotional state that is more resilient to external pressures.

On a physical level, Dhikr has tangible health benefits as well. The act of remembering Allah can significantly reduce stress-related symptoms, contributing to a calmer and more balanced physiological state. This practice promotes a positive mindset, helping individuals focus on the present moment rather than dwelling on worries. The relaxation that comes with Dhikr can also have beneficial effects on heart health, as it reduces the physical effects of stress and encourages a sense of tranquillity.

Taken as a whole, the practice of Dhikr nurtures a holistic well-being, nurturing the mind, body, and soul. It is much more than just a religious ritual; it is a way to cultivate peace, presence, and purpose in daily life. Through its powerful spiritual, emotional, and physical benefits, Dhikr offers a means of creating harmony within oneself, leading to a more fulfilling and balanced life.

## Encouragement to Integrate Dhikr into Daily Life as a Lasting Practice

Now that we understand its value, the next step is to make Dhikr a consistent part of our lives. Don't think of it as something extra to add to your schedule. Instead, weave it into your daily routine in small but meaningful ways. For example:

- Say Bismillah (In the name of Allah (SWT) before beginning anything.

- Say Alhamdulillah after every meal or when something goes well.

- Whisper Astaghfirullah (I seek forgiveness from Allah (SWT) when you feel stressed or make a mistake.

- Set aside a few minutes after each prayer to recite your favourite phrases of remembrance.

Make use of quiet moments—while walking, waiting in line, or driving—to repeat simple phrases. You'll find that these small habits, when done with sincerity, have a big impact on your heart. It's also helpful to set reminders or alarms throughout the day to pause and remember Allah (SWT). Keep a Dhikr app on your phone or carry a tasbih (prayer beads) with you. Some people even stick short phrases of Dhikr on their walls or desks as visual reminders.

Remember: the goal is not perfection but consistency. Even if you miss a day or forget, simply return to the habit without guilt. Allah (SWT) loves those who try to turn to Him again and again.

## Creating a Lasting Dhikr Habit

Building a lifelong Dhikr habit takes patience and planning. Here are some practical tips to help you stay committed:

Start Small: Begin with short phrases like SubhanAllah (SWT) or La ilaha illAllah (SWT). Make it easy and natural. Even five minutes a day is a great start.

Link Dhikr with Daily Activities: Connect Dhikr with actions you do every day—such as walking, commuting, or preparing meals. It becomes part of your rhythm.

Be Present: Try to say Dhikr with focus and meaning. Think about what the words mean. Let them sink into your heart instead of just your tongue.

Track Your Progress: Keep a Dhikr journal or use an app to track how often you remember Allah (SWT). This helps build motivation and a sense of purpose.

Surround Yourself with Reminders: Put visual cues around your home or workplace. You can even write motivational quotes or verses from the Quran that encourage remembrance.

Ask Allah (SWT) for Help: Make Dua (supplication) asking Allah (SWT) to help you remember Him often. The Prophet (PBUH) used to say: "O

# HABITUAL PEACE

Allah (SWT), help me remember You, thank You, and worship You in the best manner." (Abu Dawood)

The goal is to make Dhikr a natural part of your life—not something you have to remind yourself to do, but something you enjoy and look forward to. Over time, you'll notice a positive change in your mindset, emotions, and faith.

## Tips for Sustaining a Lifelong Commitment to Dhikr

Building a consistent and lifelong habit of Dhikr—the remembrance of Allah—is one of the most rewarding spiritual goals a person can pursue. It strengthens the heart, soothes the soul, and keeps the believer grounded in both good times and difficult ones. However, making Dhikr a lasting practice requires more than occasional effort. It requires intention, commitment, and strategic approaches that foster long-term growth.

One of the first and most powerful steps is to renew your intention regularly. In Islam, every act is valued according to the intention behind it. Over time, it's easy for routines to become automatic, even in acts of worship. That's why it's important to pause and ask yourself why you're engaging in Dhikr. Is it to check off a spiritual task from your list, or is it to deepen your connection with Allah? When your intention is clear and heartfelt—to remember Allah sincerely and seek His closeness—then even a short session of Dhikr becomes deeply meaningful. This self-check can reignite your passion and remind you of the purpose behind your remembrance.

Another helpful approach is to involve someone else in your journey. Encouraging a friend or family member to do Dhikr with you can bring motivation and accountability. When someone else is striving toward the same goal, it becomes easier to stay consistent. You can exchange reflections, remind each other gently, and even share the impact Dhikr is having on your life. This shared spiritual growth strengthens not only your habit but also your relationship with the other person. It builds a bond around something that truly matters.

If you live in a community where spiritual gatherings are available, joining a Dhikr circle can be a deeply uplifting experience. Collective remembrance has a unique energy. Hearing others mention Allah, seeing the peace on their faces, and feeling part of a group centred on the Divine can rekindle your motivation and remind you that you're not alone on this path. Even if your schedule doesn't allow for regular attendance, joining occasionally can refresh your spirit and keep you inspired.

Setting small, achievable goals is also a key to long-term success. Trying to do everything at once often leads to burnout or discouragement. Instead, choose one simple Dhikr to focus on each month. For example, you might decide to say "*Astaghfirullah*" 100 times a day for a whole month. The repetition will help you internalise it, and the steady pace will make it easier to stick with. Over time, you can rotate different phrases and gradually build a richer and more balanced routine of remembrance.

It's also valuable to take time to reflect on your progress. How has your heart changed since you started doing Dhikr more consistently? Are you more patient, more grateful, more aware of Allah's presence in your life? These reflections allow you to appreciate the spiritual benefits you've gained, which in turn encourage you to continue. Writing in a journal or simply sitting quietly with your thoughts can help you recognise the subtle yet powerful impact Dhikr is having on your mind and soul.

Sustaining any habit becomes easier when you can feel the results. The beauty of Dhikr lies in its ability to bring peace, clarity, and a sense of purpose to everyday life. The more you experience these effects, the more naturally you'll be drawn to continue. What once felt like an effort becomes a source of joy. You begin to crave the calm that comes with remembrance, especially in times of stress or uncertainty.

To make Dhikr a permanent part of your life, it's important to stay gentle with yourself. There may be days when you forget or feel too tired. Instead of giving up, treat these moments as opportunities to return with more sincerity. The goal is not perfection, but persistence. Every moment of remembrance is valuable, no matter how small it may seem.

Ultimately, a life filled with Dhikr is a life filled with light. With patience, intention, and the right strategies, you can make the remembrance of Allah (SWT) a natural and constant part of your existence. The effort you put in today will echo far beyond this world, becoming a source of reward, comfort, and closeness to your Creator for all eternity.

# Chapter Twelve

# Conclusion

Every heartbeat, every breath, every fleeting moment we experience in this world is a chance to draw closer to our Creator. As you conclude this book, remember that the journey of Dhikr does not end here—it begins anew with each sunrise, each challenge, and each quiet moment of reflection.

This path is not reserved for saints or scholars alone; it is open to every soul that longs for peace, clarity, and purpose. Whether your days are filled with noise or stillness, triumph or trial, Dhikr is your anchor—gently pulling your heart back to Allah (SWT).

You've learned that Dhikr is not a task confined to the prayer mat or the masjid. It belongs in your steps, your silence, your whispers, and your tears. It is in the steady repetition of sacred words, in the gratitude felt for blessings seen and unseen, in the surrender to divine wisdom when life doesn't go as planned. It is simple, yet infinitely profound. From a soft whisper in the stillness of dawn to a silent utterance in a crowded street, Dhikr transforms ordinary moments into acts of devotion. And when done consistently, it doesn't just soothe the soul—it reshapes it.

This transformation is not instant. It is slow and steady, like a seed nurtured over time. Some days will feel vibrant and spiritually alive, while others may feel dry and distracted. But never underestimate the value of persistence. Every effort counts. Every remembrance matters. Even when your heart feels distant, keep your tongue moist with His

# HABITUAL PEACE

name. Allah (SWT) sees your striving, and He multiplies it in ways you cannot imagine.

Let this book serve as a reminder that no matter where you are in life, Dhikr is always within reach. It doesn't require perfection, only intention. You may stumble, you may forget—but always return. Always begin again. Build habits, not just hopes. Make Dhikr part of your rhythm, until remembrance becomes your second nature. When you walk, remember. When you wait, remember. When you weep, remember. And when you rejoice, remember. In every state, let your soul echo the praises of its Lord.

Know that what you are building through Dhikr is far greater than inner peace. You are cultivating a heart that remains connected to Allah (SWT) through the highs and the lows. You are preparing your soul for the eternal life to come. And you are creating a life that carries meaning far beyond the visible world. In the end, this practice will not only shape who you are in this dunya—it will define who you become in the Akhirah.

May your journey with Dhikr be a lifelong one. May it bring you light in your grave, shade on the Day of Judgment, and joy when you finally meet the One you've been remembering all along. This is the gift of habitual peace. Treasure it. Live it. And may it lead you to the ultimate success—contentment in this life, and eternal reward in the next. Ameen.

# Find Out More

**Website:** www.barakahinbusiness.com

**Socials:** @barakahinbusiness

If you enjoyed this book, kindly leave a review to help expand our reach so others may benefit also.